# JOY IN EVERY CIRCUMSTANCE

A thirty-day study

in

Paul's letter
to the

# Philippians

Pastor Jack Abeelen

Published by Morningstar Christian Chapel
ISBN-13: 978-0-9842943-2-9
ISBN-10: 0-9842943-2-5



All scriptures are taken from the New King James Version of the Bible, unless otherwise indicated. Translational emendations, amplifications, and paraphrases are by the author.

Additional copies of this book are available by contacting:

Morningstar Christian Chapel
16241 Leffingwell Road, Whittier, California, 90603

The Chapel Store
562-943-0357

# JOY IN EVERY CIRCUMSTANCE
## Paul's Letter to the Philippians

By Pastor Jack Abeelen

# Contents

Note to the Reader:

This book has been divided into 30 one-a-day chapters. At the end of each chapter you will find a section (pictured below) where you can chart your progress as well as write a short note to yourself detailing how you plan to apply the day's lesson to your life.

***Example***

❑ Day One Complete – Date: _________________________________________

Application: ____________________________________________________

____________________________________________________________

____________________________________________________________

____________________________________________________________

# Introduction

# Introduction

Samuel Clemens, whose pen name was Mark Twain, was a humorist by trade. Yet his life story is that of a sad man. When his daughter died of epilepsy at a very young age, he was too saddened by her death to attend her funeral. In fact, he said to a friend that the only thing he ever envied of anyone is that they could die. Quite a somber outlook for a man known for his humor and wit. We're told by the prophet Isaiah that Jesus was a man of sorrows who was acquainted with grief (Isaiah 53:3). Yet as you walk with Jesus through the Gospels you would be hard-pressed to find Him sad very often. What you find instead is great joy in the face of a cruel cross and a difficult crowd. "These things I have spoken to you, that My joy may remain in you, and that your joy may be full," He told His disciples (John 15:11).

So, on the one hand is a man who is paid to make people laugh – yet his heart within breaks every day. On the other hand is God, who comes to a world that hates Him and in which most will reject Him. Yet He comes to die in their place so their sins may be forgiven and He is filled with joy from morning until night.

In Psalm 16:11, David writes, "You will show me the path of life; In Your presence is fullness of joy; At Your right hand are pleasures forevermore." Do you believe God's will for you today is that you might be filled with joy? I believe it is. God's will is that your entire life be filled with His joy. Why then don't we see more saints of God truly walking in His joy? More often than not, Christians seem to have had their joy ripped off. As a result, they wander through life much like those in the world who don't know the Lord – without much hope. They see everything from a negative viewpoint. Oh, once in a while they'll have a good day – but then they're quickly discouraged again. What took away their joy and how can they get it back?

Many answers can be found in this letter Paul wrote from a jail cell in Rome about 62 AD, where he was being held to await a verdict on his trial before Nero. If it went badly, he would be beheaded. If it went well, he might actually be released. But he had no clear insight as to how this was all going to work out. He had given it his best and now committed it to the Lord. So he is sitting and waiting and wondering and praying…

As he waits, he receives a messenger named Epaphroditus who has been sent to Rome to give him a special offering from a church in the city of Philippi. It had been Paul's first missionary stop in Europe. It had seen humble beginnings and much persecution but God had begun a glorious work. Paul here writes to them from less than ideal circumstances and, of all things, he chooses to write to them on the topic of the joy of the Lord! Really? Really! Let's take a look.

# Background
# Day One

*Paul and Barnabas also remained in Antioch, teaching and preaching the word of the Lord, with many others also. Then after some days Paul said to Barnabas, "Let us now go back and visit our brethren in every city where we have preached the word of the Lord, and see how they are doing."*

*—Acts 15:35-36*

Both from this verse and from church history, we learn that Paul and Barnabas, having returned from their first missionary journey, would spend the next several years teaching and preaching in their local home church in Antioch. Ministering to the saints and preaching to the lost, they were serving the Lord in a very real way. It was in that place of serving that God began to stir Paul's heart. If you want to know the kind of people God can use, mark this down: God uses people who are busy serving Him. Paul and Barnabas had been on the road for quite some time. Yet when they came home they stepped right back into serving at the local body level. They weren't above it. It wasn't too much for them. It was the place God had for them. And it was from there that Paul, serving the Lord with Barnabas and many others, began to feel his heart moved by God.

Paul never was a guy who was very comfortable in the "comfort zone." He was a man of God with a view and a vision of the lost in the world that very few folks seem to have – and he hungered to be out there. I don't know if one of his arguments for going was, as we read in verse 35, that there were plenty of guys ministering in Antioch anyway. But I do know he had a tremendous passion for the lost and for the churches!

If you are going to be used by God in the world to reach the lost, you can begin by asking God to give you the kind of passion and love for souls that moved Paul. In his second letter to the Corinthians, he said one reason for his heart for those who did not know the Lord was the mercy God had shown him. (2 Corinthians 4:1). I would think that your greatest motivation for reaching others with Jesus' love is the fact that He loves you. Paul went on to say to the Corinthians in chapter 5 that it was the love of Christ that constrained him that he couldn't help from serving. That is why; sitting in a very successful, growing church that had lots of things going for it, Paul's greatest concern was to see how others were doing.

In all honesty, I don't know of any class in any school that you can take to develop passion for the lost. I think it only comes when you realize and understand the things God has done for you. You've probably seen people get involved in ministry for reasons other than a passion for the Lord. After a while, the things of God are no longer exciting and the newness wears off. The difficulty of the task and length of the commitment weed out the dispassionate. However, if your passion is based on what you've been delivered from, I can't imagine anything that would turn that off in your life. Paul said to Barnabas, "This place is fine. They've got all kinds of guys. We've got to go back into the field to see how the saints are doing."

Because he was in the Word daily, serving in ministry, and living a life of thanksgiving and prayer, Paul had great passion. God, give us passion like Paul's! Not only did Paul have the right passion, but he also had the right priorities. I point that out because the long-term view for evangelism correctly focuses itself on the saints, not on the world. The best thing you can do in evangelism is to make sure the disciples are growing – that they are being well-taught and well-fed.

Paul's longing was to go and establish those in the faith that he had led to the Lord on the first trip. He wanted to help them in their walk. Why? Because healthy sheep will always produce other healthy sheep! Get people walking with God and the natural result is that they are going to want to tell others about what God has done for them.

Most of the time, the work of evangelism is done by the church, not in the church. If you look at the letters Paul would later write, you find that he would constantly be in prayer for the young saints from whom he was absent for longer periods of time than he was present. Nearly half a dozen of his letters begin with him saying, "Every time I pray, I make mention of you. I'm always thinking about how you're doing." For the Ephesians, he prayed that they would understand the depth and the height, the length and the width of the love God had for them (Ephesians 3:17-18). To the Philippian church, he wrote, "I thank my God upon every remembrance of you, always in every prayer of mine making request for you all with joy, for your fellowship in the gospel from the first day until now" (Philippians 1:3-5). He would write to the Thessalonians that, though he was absent from them, he always made mention of them in his prayers (1 Thessalonians 1:2-3). Paul had the right passion but he also had the right priorities or the right application of His passions, as He sought to disciple those he had led to the Lord. He was concerned about their growth.

If I asked you who you are discipling, what would you say? Who are you teaching the things God has taught you? Who are you caring for and praying for daily? Or who is discipling you? Who do you look up to? Paul spent his time with folks who needed to grow and he took a real interest in how they were doing spiritually. In whose life are you spiritually involved? The best method of evangelism has always been personal, a one-on-one reaching out to the lost and helping them know and then grow in Jesus Christ. Jesus rarely spoke to large crowds in comparison to the time He spent with 12 men – 11 of whom would turn the world upside down.

So as his second missionary trip was being planned, Paul desires to return to those he had reached his first time out. Years later, according to Acts 18, Paul on his third trip would do the exact same thing – go revisit those whom God had begun a work in and through. He stuck with the work and taught his disciples to do the same. He said to the Colossians, "Him we preach, warning every man and teaching every man in all wisdom, that we may present every man perfect in Christ Jesus." (Colossians 1:28) Of Epaphras, he said to the Colossians that he was one who had labored fervently in prayer that they would stand perfect and complete in the will of God (Colossians 4:12). It's not enough to share your faith. Paul shared his life with a view toward helping others to stand in faith. The church should always be very involved in discipleship, new believer classes, and the instruction of the young so that they might be established and go forth to bear much fruit.

❑ Day One Complete – Date: _______________________________________

Application: _________________________________________________

_________________________________________________________

_________________________________________________________

_________________________________________________________

# Background
# Day Two

*Now Barnabas was determined to take with them John called Mark. But Paul insisted that they should not take with them the one who had departed from them in Pamphylia, and had not gone with them to the work. Then the contention became so sharp that they parted from one another. And so Barnabas took Mark and sailed to Cyprus; but Paul chose Silas and departed, being commended by the brethren to the grace of God. And he went through Syria and Cilicia, strengthening the churches.*

*—Acts 15:37-41*

Along with having a right passion and setting the right priorities, we also want to be sure as we go out, and send others out, that we have chosen the right people. Are we sending those whom God has called? We must be in tune with what God wants to do. Paul and Barnabas were, no doubt, the best of friends. They had accomplished more together in the Lord than most friends would hope to accomplish in a lifetime. And yet when it came to this second trip, an issue arose regarding Barnabas' nephew, John Mark, who had bailed out early on the first trip. Paul and Barnabas needed a helper who could go ahead of them to find housing and food, and sometimes gather bail money. (It seemed they were always in jail!) They needed an administrative manager – one who could carry the bags, book passage on the ships, and help out in general. But the work wasn't easy. Pamphylia had not been a nice place. So John Mark, being a young guy, had gone home, no doubt due to fear and hardship. It had left Paul and Barnabas short-handed and added yet another burden.

John Mark lived in Jerusalem with his mother, Mary, Barnabas' sister. He had recently seen Paul and Barnabas again as they had been asked to come up to the Jerusalem council, which was addressing salvation and the Gentiles (Acts 15). Maybe John Mark got wind of how Paul had reacted to his leaving from Barnabas and he may have said to his uncle, "If you ever go again, call on me. Give me another shot. I won't blow it next time. I'm ready to serve the Lord for sure." What convinces me of that is Barnabas' determination to give him another chance as mentioned by Luke in Acts 15:37 where the word determined is an imperfect tense verb meaning Barnabas had made up his mind earlier but was just now suggesting it to Paul. Barnabas was intent on giving Junior another shot. He was going to disciple him. He was determined to help him.

But he also knew Paul wouldn't like the idea. The collision could be seen coming a mile away. Acts 15:38 tells us Paul was having none of it. He was a very courageous man who viewed John Mark as a liability. The road was going to be tough; the work was too important. "I don't want to baby-sit this guy. I know he's your little nephew, but we can't take him with us. We need tough men with sound convictions."

Acts 15:39 says that a sharp contention grew between them. These are strong Greek words that would imply that they didn't just argue, they yelled loudly at each other! I can hear the discussion – Barnabas saying to Paul, "Hey, man, if I hadn't helped you, the disciples wouldn't have even talked to you. You owe me, dude!" And Paul answering, "Oh, yeah. You're Mister Big Shot who followed Peter when James' boys came to Galatia. There you were, eating with Gentiles – until they showed up, and you acted like you didn't care about the Gentiles. I had to put you right, didn't I? You need me, pal. You might be a supportive man but, doctrinally, you need me." Wow!

The result was not unexpected; the mission team split up. You don't read of handshakes or hugs or high fives. You just read of two strong men in the Lord with convictions they both felt were too important to let go. So Barnabas would take his young nephew to his hometown of Cyprus, where he and Paul had first found God's blessing. Paul, meanwhile, chooses Silas from the men who are ministering at the church in Antioch and heads north toward Galatia where he will retrace his steps from east to west and visit the churches he had visited and helped establish.

What interests me, from a practical standpoint, is how God can work through two godly men who totally disagree and are both right. John Mark was a failure the first time out. Paul didn't necessarily have to believe he'd do better this time. Barnabas was right in standing with a weak young man who loved the Lord and needed more than a bit of encouragement to be all God intended for him. Paul was task-oriented. Barnabas was very much interested in the individual. John Mark would develop very well under Barnabas' leadership. He would later join Peter and, hearing Peter's recollections of the days of Jesus, would eventually write the Gospel of Mark. Years later as Paul was awaiting execution in Rome, he would write in 2 Timothy 4:11, "Only Luke is with me. Get Mark and bring him with you, for he is useful to me for ministry." Paul came to see John Mark as a great asset, but it would take some time and the devotion of men like Barnabas and Peter.

I would say if you're a John Mark and feel you have failed the Lord, be encouraged because God isn't finished with you either. And even if some like Paul might write you off, there will be plenty of people like Barnabas who will not. Those Pauls might be right. You have failed; you blew it; you messed up; you came up short; you swung and missed. But God knew all of those things beforehand. So hang in there because He has great plans for you. You can get up again and discover God's best.

On the other hand, Paul's new missionary partner Silas was absolutely the right man for this trip. He was Jewish with Roman citizenship which he would certainly need for the places God was going to send them; far beyond where they had yet imagined. And from all that we gather from this trip, just like Paul, he was also tough as nails – both would sing worship songs after they were beat up and left for dead. John Mark might have gone home again, but not Silas. He instead sang another chorus as the blood flowed from his wounds. Silas was the right choice, and time would show that as, without hesitancy, he walked time and again into the midst of hell to preach the Gospel.

These verses and this conflict between two men of God should teach us that there is room for dispute in the Body of Christ. I don't think we always have to totally agree – as long as we don't allow things to get personal. People in urban areas, where our church is located, can be prone to church-hopping. Because of the number of good churches available, folks tend to change churches for the most feeble of excuses. They run from issues they ought to resolve simply by leaving for another place. Others, however, both come and go, led by the Holy Spirit within their hearts. I love watching God raise up servants in the body here and love seeing God send other saints to serve elsewhere. It is, after all, His church, not mine. It's not a personality contest. It's not a competition. It's the work of God's Spirit in us and through us and with us. The key is to hear from God and follow Him as these two giants in the faith did.

In the end, Paul and Silas were sent out by the church and accountable to the local body. I presume they were supported financially by them as well. And, more importantly, they were supported prayerfully. I would hate to begin to tell you the tragic stories of those who go out to the mission field on their own – without much accountability or prayerful support. Many die on the vine because missions work is to be an extension of the local body, which benefits all.

*Then he came to Derbe and Lystra. And behold, a certain disciple was there, named Timothy, the son of a certain Jewish woman who believed, but his father was Greek. He was well spoken of by the brethren who were at Lystra and Iconium. Paul wanted to have him go on with him. And he took him and circumcised him because of the Jews who were in that region, for they all knew that his father was Greek.*

*—Acts 16:1-3*

As Paul and Silas went forth, recommended by the brethren to God's grace, they first headed for Syria and Cilicia – the Galatia churches. They had the right passion, the right priorities, and now they had the right people. Next they would need the right plans.

The first time Paul had been to Derbe, he and Barnabas had found great success as well as some needed rest. It was one of the few places where no one beat them up or chased them out of town. Yet when they later came to Lystra, God had healed a lame man and the people thought Paul and Barnabas were gods who had come down to them from the heavens. When Paul set them straight, in their embarrassment and anger, the people stoned him and then drug him outside of the city leaving him to die. As they arrive in Lystra, Paul, to his great joy, discovers the church there is doing great and bearing fruit – a solid proof to Paul that God was really at work here. Amen!

It is here, at the beginning of their journey that Paul comes across Timothy. Raised as a Jew, Timothy had apparently received Jesus when Paul had been here the first time. The reason we believe this is that Paul calls Timothy his beloved son in the faith several times (1 Corinthians 4:17; Philippians 2:22; 1 Timothy 1:2). His grandmother, Lois, and his mother, Eunice, had raised Timothy. From childhood, he'd been schooled in the Scriptures, but apparently his Greek father had enough influence to keep him from being circumcised. The word "was" in Acts 16:1 is in the imperfect tense implying Timothy's father had died by this time. Since Paul's previous visit, not only had Timothy begun to grow in the Lord but now he was in a position where he had a good reputation in both Lystra and the neighboring town of Iconium. Paul would later tell Timothy that an important qualification for church leadership was a good reputation (1 Timothy 3:2). Timothy had that and Paul wanted to take him along, no doubt as a replacement for John Mark.

In fact, Timothy would become Paul's favorite disciple. He would write to the Philippians, "For I have no one like-minded, who will sincerely care for your state. For all seek their own, not the things which are of Christ Jesus. But you know his proven character, that as a son with his father he served with me in the gospel" (Philippians 2:20-22).

Paul asks Timothy to join with them and Timothy quickly agrees because he also had a passion for the lost. We're told in 2 Timothy 1:6 that the church here came together to pray for Timothy, laying hands upon him and asking God to equip him with the gifts of the Spirit. The team had grown to three. There was only one hitch: Timothy would need to be circumcised, as ministry amongst the Jews would require it.

*"You sure you don't want me to just join a fraternity or something?" Timothy must have wondered. It may seem odd that Paul would require this of Timothy – especially in light of the decision made at the Jerusalem meeting that practices of Jewish law were not to be laid upon Gentiles. However, for Paul, it was a matter of ministry. He always went to the Jews first. "For though I am free from all men, I have made myself a servant to all, that I might win the more; and to the Jews I became as a Jew, that I might win Jews; to those who are under the law, as under the law, that I might win those who are under the law; to those who*

*are without law, as without law (not being without law toward God, but under law toward Christ), that I might win those who are without law; to the weak I became as weak, that I might win the weak. I have become all things to all men, that I might by all means save some. Now this I do for the gospel's sake, that I may be partaker of it with you. Do you not know that those who run in a race all run, but one receives the prize? Run in such a way that you may obtain it. And everyone who competes for the prize is temperate in all things. Now they do it to obtain a perishable crown, but we for an imperishable crown. Therefore I run thus: not with uncertainty. Thus I fight: not as one who beats the air. But I discipline my body and bring it into subjection, lest, when I have preached to others, I myself should become disqualified."*

*1 Corinthians 9:19-27*

One principle for missions is that it requires right planning: know the beliefs of the area to which you are going and do as much as possible to fit in without crossing a moral or theological line. Later on, when Paul would be asked about circumcising Titus, he would say it wasn't necessary because Titus was a Gentile and he was reaching out to Gentiles. Timothy, on the other hand, was at least half Jewish and Paul wanted to show the Jews respect for their position and for the type that was given to point them to God. Timothy went the extra mile as he headed out for parts unknown to serve the Lord.

# Day Three

❏ **Day Two Complete** – Date: _______________________________

Application: _______________________________

_______________________________

_______________________________

_______________________________

# Background
# Day Three

*And as they went through the cities, they delivered to them the decrees to keep, which were determined by the apostles and elders at Jerusalem. So the churches were strengthened in the faith, and increased in number daily.*

*—Acts 16:4-5*

Luke covers the next several months of ministry in just two verses but in them we discover another key ingredient to consider: we need the right presentation. Their preaching was based upon the decision the apostles had made when they had met in Jerusalem – namely that it wasn't following the law that would bring salvation, but only the grace of Jesus, available to all men, that saves! So as Paul preached salvation by grace, the churches increased in number and were rooted, established, and grounded in their faith in Jesus. The growth came simply because they were teaching the Bible and the Word of God was reaching those hungry to know Him.

How people need to hear the Word of God! The numbers always come when the Word of God goes out. Don't ever forget that. You must have the right presentation and the formula is always the same: teach the Word; the people will be established; and the numbers will grow. Some churches focus only on how to get people in – sometimes in very absurd ways. I once took some classes on church growth and the things we were taught on how to bring people into the building were phenomenal. It was deceitful. They wanted you to become a slick salesman rather than a minister of the Gospel of Jesus Christ.

Today they have a name for it: seeker-friendly churches. They try to be what people like and have confidence in things other than the power of God's Word to save. Call it what you will, any trust in any method that sets aside the Word of God is bound to fail. It won't last because it doesn't meet the needs of the heart to be forgiven, saved, and delivered by the grace found in Jesus. You might be able to draw a crowd and pack them in with your less-than-Gospel presentation – but you can also pack them in for a football game. Numbers are not proof, changed lives are. And only the Gospel changes lives. Numbers will follow the teaching of the Word because changed lives draw attention!

A Korean pastor came by recently looking for a place to bring his congregation. "How fast do you grow?" he asked. We began to talk about the fact that the growth of the church here hasn't been dramatic but it has been consistent – somewhere between 10 to 15 percent each year. God is faithful to His Word. We haven't changed anything. I think there are a lot of things we could do to get people here faster but are lives going to change? That's the issue. Look again at Acts 16:5. The churches were established in their faith by the teaching of God's Word and the numbers increased daily.

> *Now when they had gone through Phrygia and the region of Galatia, they were forbidden by the Holy Spirit to preach the word in Asia. After they had come to Mysia, they tried to go into Bithynia, but the Spirit did not permit them. So passing by Mysia, they came down to Troas.*
>
> *—Acts 16:6-8*

There is one last "right" that we would like to mention along with what we have seen so far and that is the boys ended up in the "right" place. Having covered all the familiar territory, the question soon became, "Where do we go from here?"

Certainly waiting on the Lord to direct your path can

be both a frustrating and challenging experience. From this portion of Scripture and the experience of Paul and his team, it seems you can find yourself entirely in the will of God and still not be sure whether you're headed in the right direction. If you follow Paul's attempts to find God's path, you'll see how he went down every possible road only to find closed doors at each one. Paul and his team might have sat up nights, wondering aloud, "What is God doing, anyway? Where is He when we need Him most?"

It comforts me to know that there aren't always easy methods of determining the will of God right away. Here were three Spirit-filled men of God yet none of them were saying, "I think we should go here." They didn't seem to have it clearly figured out. As I read this, my impression is that Paul wanted to stop just about everywhere he headed. He went west – nothing. He tried to go a little to the north – nothing. He finally heads directly north but if he stays on that road long enough, he'll end up in the Aegean Sea. He's out on the mission field commissioned by the Lord. He's got the right passion, the right priorities, and the right people with him. He had taken the right precautions and has been giving the right presentation. He just didn't have the right place to go, not yet. But never say die, Paul, God is still with you.

Some commentators argue that the way God stopped Paul from going into all of these places was by allowing him to become very sick. Their reason primarily is that in verse 10, we'll see Luke begin to use the third person pronoun "we" instead of "they." In other words, at this point, Luke joins the team. Luke, being a physician, drove some scholars to conclude that Paul needed him because every time Paul tried to go somewhere, God slowed him down via illness for months at a time. Whether that's true or not, I don't know. I do know that on his third trip out, these places that are named as being forbidden by the Spirit, are the very places God will send Paul.

*And a vision appeared to Paul in the night. A man*

*of Macedonia stood and pleaded with him, saying, "Come over to Macedonia and help us." Now after he had seen the vision, immediately we sought to go to Macedonia, concluding that the Lord had called us to preach the gospel to them.*

*—Acts 16:9-10*

As the land ran out and the sea appeared, Paul must have gone to bed with the same prayer for direction on his heart. This night, however, his concerns would be alleviated, because God's will would become abundantly clear – He was calling them to Europe. Convinced this was indeed His will, Paul, Silas, Timothy, and Luke set off immediately. Their first stop of consequence would be the city of Philippi, where God will give to us the story of three significant conversions that would become the basis for the church that would be planted there.

*Therefore, sailing from Troas, we ran a straight course to Samothrace, and the next day came to Neapolis, and from there to Philippi, which is the foremost city of that part of Macedonia, a colony. And we were staying in that city for some days. And on the Sabbath day we went out of the city to the riverside, where prayer was customarily made; and we sat down and spoke to the women who met there.*

*—Acts 16:11-13*

Troas was previously called the city of Troy. Samothracia is an island still in existence today with a 500-foot hill dominating its center. In Paul's day, there were numerous religions practiced on this island. Paul, however, didn't see fit to stay there because God had specifically called him to the mainland, to Macedonia. There were needs on the island but for now God had other plans for Paul and the team. We today face many needs as well but we will never meet them all.

However, if we commit ourselves to the ones God sets before us, He will meet every need in His time.

Notice Luke writes in verse 11 that they got there on a straight course – a nautical term meaning to run with the wind. This trip was a pretty quick one – 150 miles sailing in only two days. But lest you think easy sailing is proof that you are in the will of God, the very struggle they had to get to this step of the journey should tell you otherwise. Later, in Acts 16:20, the boys will try this trip again and it will take the better part of a week. Yet they were right where God wanted them then as well.

Be careful when you decide that, because things are easy, it must be the Lord at work. We must judge based on His peace in our hearts, for the easy route might also be the wrong one. The key is to find where God is going and then go with Him whether easy or hard. I personally think this trip went easy because the Lord had mercy on the head of Paul which had banged against everything trying to figure out where to go!

Ten miles or so from Cavalla today lay the ruins of Philippi. It is along the Via Ignatia, the old Roman road, remnants of which are still in existence. Paul and the boys would have to travel up this road 10 miles or so before they came to Philippi, which had been named after Alexander the Great's father, Philip of Macedon. It was here at Philippi that Anthony and Octavian (who later changed his name to Augustus, the Caesar ruling when Jesus was born) fought Brutus and Cassius following the death of Julius Caesar. The city had a long Roman history and was well known to all.

Philippi was a port city and Luke writes that it was a colony. Colonization was the way the Romans controlled huge areas of land and great numbers of people. They accomplished this by converting cities that were strategically desirable – due to major highways, a good water supply, farming potential, or marketing location – to mini-Roman towns. With the offer of free land and tax-free status, the Roman government lured retired soldiers to relocate into these strategic towns and become the local government. There was no voting – just rules mandated by Caesar. In this manner, control was achieved and these cities became "little Rome" all over the empire. Those born in these colonies were given the privilege of being Roman citizens without the cost of purchasing that status, as everyone else was required to do.

You might recall that Paul was born in the colony of Tarsus and given this free citizenship, which came in handy more than once as he was serving the Lord (Acts 22:27-28). Most people longed to live in a colony like this because it afforded both them and their children certain privileges. Yet in reality, they were still captives to the Roman Empire. Philippi, being such a city, would tell us that many retired Roman soldiers lived there and strict Roman law controlled that life.

We're told in verse 12 that Paul and his team took a few days to get their bearings here. Four men, filled with the Spirit, tired, and yet ready and excited to present the Gospel of Jesus to the people of Europe. They believed God had sent them here, but they were not sure what came next. God often works this way. He calls us and, as we follow Him, we arrive only to await further instructions. One step at a time!

We know from Jewish practice that wherever there were 10 adult Jewish men in a city, a synagogue was built. The synagogue was the center of Jewish life in many ways. As a place of instruction, worship, and even social interaction, a synagogue was built for even the smallest Jewish community. But with no synagogue found in Philippi, Paul and the boys wondered where to begin. So for days they walked and sought God to show them what to do. I think sometimes we are under the misconception that if God is with us, things just click 1, 2, 3. But all of us know by experience that is hardly the case. Paul was right where he was supposed to be and God wasn't speaking all that much.

Over time, the men hear of a prayer meeting customarily held on the Sabbath outside of town by the river. Though we do not know what Paul expected to find (I know my expectations would have been fairly high after receiving a vision to go there!), I can't believe finding a few ladies sitting together in prayer was Paul's hope for the Gospel coming to Europe. Yet that is exactly what he found and his response was one that said his eyes were on the Lord, that in things small or great, he would faithfully serve Him. Zechariah 4:10a says, "For who has despised the day of small things?" We would do well to remember this as we set out to serve God in a big way. These smaller opportunities for faithfulness hone our hearts and uncover our true motives and intentions. It is the times when the excitement won't bring you back, but the cause will; times when the crowds don't excite you, but the Lord does; times when the event doesn't move you, but the Holy Spirit does, that are the most valuable. Learn this truth well: if God is going to do great things through your life, they must first be accomplished in your life.

So, contrary to the custom of the Pharisees who would not speak to women because they were viewed as inferior, Paul began to share with them the hope he had found in Jesus, the Messiah. He would share with them the things he would later write to the Ephesians and Colossians – that the Gentiles that were afar off had been brought close by the blood of Christ and that both Jews and Gentiles would be brought together as one. He would have shared with them the grace of God and the freedom available for them in His Son, who died and rose again.

# Day Three

❑ **Day Three Complete – Date:** ________________________________________

Application: _________________________________________________

_______________________________________________________

_______________________________________________________

_______________________________________________________

# Background
# Day Four

*Now a certain woman named Lydia heard us. She was a seller of purple from the city of Thyatira, who worshiped God. The Lord opened her heart to heed the things spoken by Paul. And when she and her household were baptized, she begged us, saying, "If you have judged me to be faithful to the Lord, come to my house and stay." So she persuaded us.*

*—Acts 16:14-15*

One of the ladies to whom God now directs our attention actually hailed from Thyatira, a city in an area the Holy Spirit had restricted Paul from going to earlier. Lydia was probably not her name since that was the place in Thyatira where she had lived. So it probably is better translated, "a certain woman from Lydia." Thyatira, in Asia Minor, was known for its expensive dyes obtained from shellfish and used for fine clothing. It would seem that this lady was a representative of a company where these dyes were manufactured and that she had moved to Philippi, where she owned a large home and was apparently very successful.

We are told in verse 14 that she was a worshipper of God. In Greek, it literally reads "a God-fearer" and it is a term applied to Gentiles who had converted but hadn't fully embraced all aspects of Judaism. Like Cornelius and the Ethiopian eunuch, this woman from Lydia grew up worshipping lots of gods but learned from the Jews that there was only one God. Converting to Judaism would not have been an easy move on her part as evidenced by the small group gathered outside of town to pray. They didn't have a fancy building or much honor. But God heard her prayer and opened her heart.

That is a valuable insight to remember when you share your faith with others because, in reality, we can never hope to reach the lost with the good news of Jesus simply because we are good speakers, put things very logically, make moving emotional appeals, or are able to drive people to a response. All of those abilities are absolutely worthless until God, by His Spirit, works in the heart. We are lost in sin and dead in them and it's hard to get a dead man to pay attention. It is the work of the Spirit through the Word of God, which convinces, convicts, and opens the eyes of those dead in sin.

Paul said to the Ephesians 2:1-6 that we all used to walk according to the course of this world. We were dead in our trespasses and sins and that is where God found us. I mean, did you really think you would ever get saved? Everyone that knew me figured I would be the last person to get saved. But look what God can do! God used Paul but it was a work of the Spirit. So as you go out and share with others, you must rely on God's Word. You must depend upon the work of His Spirit. And then you can rest; knowing you have done your best and that you have shared what the Lord has given you.

I can't count the number of times I have talked to new believers who say, "I talked to my parents about the Lord but I think I messed it up."

"What do you mean you messed it up?" I ask.

"Oh, I got mad and then I forgot a verse I was going to tell them." Or, "I told them where it was and it wasn't there! Now I don't think they will ever believe me."

Rest assured you cannot really mess up that which only God can accomplish. Besides, God uses goofs. If you don't believe that, look in a mirror! If you didn't mess up, now that would be amazing. That you mess up is normal.

This woman from Lydia listened to Paul and the boys and out of this group of gathered women, she is the one who hears the message of Jesus, opens her heart to Him, and receives Him as her Lord and Savior. Years later, a church would spring up in her hometown of Thyatira, to which Jesus will write a letter in Revelation 2. Maybe she even had a part in it being planted. Look here at how God works, how He had prepared the way for her to be saved. She was doing great in her business in Lydia, but the business apparently wanted to expand. So she, being a good saleswoman, was commissioned to move to Philippi. Paul tried to go to her hometown but, through closed doors, the Lord said, "I don't want you to go there." "Where should I go?" Paul asked. "To Europe," the Lord eventually answered. "Why?" Paul must have wondered. "So you can talk to this woman from Thyatira who is sitting by a river in Philippi, praying to know Me."

The Lord put this whole thing together. You might not realize that as you are in the middle of it all but here, looking back, you can easily see God's hand in every step.

We read in verse 15 that she and her whole family were baptized. Apparently she went home where her family observed her conversion and testimony. No doubt an undetermined amount of time passed and eventually her family and household servants all came to know Jesus themselves as well. This isn't the first household in the Bible to get saved and it isn't the last, either. Cornelius and his whole family came to Christ in Acts 10. And toward the end of this chapter, the Philippian jailor sees his whole family get right with God literally overnight. Later, in Acts 18, Crispus, the head of the synagogue in Corinth, hearing Paul share, is saved and, in the process of time, so is his entire family. It all starts with one, doesn't it?

From my experience as a pastor, once one person is saved, the rest of the family had better watch out! More often than not, that's where a new believer's work begins. It's not necessarily where the first fruit will come from, but it's where the calling of God leads us. I'll see a son get saved, then the mom follow – and before you know it, her husband is sitting next to her in church. At baptisms where I often find new believers, young in the Lord, I will hear things like: "I was saved 6 weeks ago and last Sunday I brought my husband to church with me and he accepted the Lord." So awesome! You can never hear that too often!

If you are the only believer in your family, you should be very encouraged. You have a great opportunity and responsibility. Through prayer, lots of work, lots of light shining in dark places, lots of tolerance and love and patience and faith, God's work through His Word will be accomplished. The woman from Lydia told her family, as did Crispus and the jailer. Cornelius didn't have to tell them because he gathered them together to hear Peter. Praise the Lord when He puts you in that place! This woman couldn't prove her conversion in one day. But over a period of time, the whole family saw and believed in Jesus and Paul and his team was so thrilled.

Now she invites them to stay in her house with the words, "If you have judged me to be faithful, come." In other words, "If you believe God has really done a work in me, if I'm not going to be an offense to your message or your ministry, come and stay with us." What could Paul say to that? She's a very good saleswoman! No wonder her business was doing so well! And she was indeed a great witness to her family.

*Now it happened, as we went to prayer, that a certain slave girl possessed with a spirit of divination met us, who brought her masters much profit by fortune-telling.*

*—Acts 16:16*

If the first conversion was that of a high-society, high-end couture clothing line saleswoman, in verse 16 we turn to the opposite end of the spectrum. Notice that neither is a problem for the Lord because He can reach you no matter where you live.

In this account, we're given an interesting picture of life in Paul's day. One of the grave injustices at the time was that, according to estimates, as much as 30 percent of the populations in the Roman Empire were slaves. I point that out to you because neither Peter nor Paul, Timothy nor Luke, Mark nor John – not even Jesus – ever went out of their way to say one word about the problem of slavery. They didn't march; they didn't picket; they didn't raise funds to try to obliterate it; they didn't run political campaigns. Yet all of them would have hated the very thought of slavery. It was a dirty word to the Jewish people certainly and yet they lived with it throughout all of the New Testament times. However none of them addressed social issues. They chose instead to deal with the spiritual causes behind them and used their time to tell people how they could be saved, believing that if enough people were saved, slavery would no longer be desired.

In like manner, I believe that the primary call of the church today is not to march for social justice. We are rather called to preach the Gospel of Jesus. If the heart is wicked, the legislation of righteousness won't last. People say, "We've got to do something about the drug problem." We sure do: preach to people that Jesus is Lord!

What got me off drugs? I got saved. I loved getting high and no amount of people telling me drugs were bad for me could stop me. I couldn't have cared less if doing drugs was bad for me. I loved it – until Jesus changed my life. The alcoholic that quits drinking doesn't quit because he hates throwing up. Even throwing up blood won't stop him. But Jesus will. Want to get rid of pornography? Preach the Gospel. Abortion? We're going to stop it when enough people love Jesus enough to love their kids. Until then, the world is going to rush itself to hell, which is why we are in the world and not of it. You don't solve spiritual issues with social action.

Though Paul never said a word about slavery, he knew how to deal with this poor slave woman. You know what changed her life and set her free? Not Paul saying, "It's a good thing I was sent here. I'm going to start a social action committee." No, it was the Gospel. The answer for each problem is the same: people need to meet Jesus and He'll change their lives. That's your testimony, isn't it?

Here was a woman possessed, owned, and enslaved. Yet the owners of this young girl saw her only as a meal ticket. She shared demonic insights for which people were willing to pay. The devil can use fortune-tellers. That is why the Bible tells us to stay away from them. Satan loves mysticism, spiritism, and religion because these keep people from walking by faith. Be careful of the wolves in "psychic network" clothing that seek only to profit from you at $3.95 a minute.

*This girl followed Paul and us, and cried out, saying, "These men are the servants of the Most High God, who proclaim to us the way of salvation." And this she did for many days.*

*—Acts 16:17-18a*

Although the slave girl's declaration was somewhat true, it was also deceptive. "The Most High God" is the title the Jews used for Jehovah. But it's also exactly the same word the Greeks used for Zeus. She actually declared that Paul and his men proclaimed a way of salvation not the only way.

As you go through the Gospels, you will find demons springing up and saying to Jesus, "What have we to do with You, Son of the most High God?" Jesus would always silence them quickly. He never tolerated their speaking for very long. And the reason is obvious: He had come to destroy the works of the devil, not set him up in a new position as a herald for Jesus. The church doesn't need worldly ways or worldly people to get the work of God done. The Holy Spirit will build the church and the gates of hell will not prevail against her.

❑ Day Four Complete – Date: _______________________________________

Application: ___________________________________________________

_____________________________________________________

_____________________________________________________

_____________________________________________________

# Background
## Day Five

*... But Paul, greatly annoyed, turned and said to the spirit, "I command you in the name of Jesus Christ to come out of her." And he came out that very hour.*
*—Acts 16:18b*

At some point, Paul spoke out. I am not sure why Paul waited so long. Maybe he didn't immediately discern this was demonic activity. He certainly needed the Lord's direction in how to deal with this matter but he didn't appear to receive it right away.

God has given us tremendous power in His name. Greater is He that is in us than he that is in the world (1 John 4:4) but it has to be at His discretion that we would take a step or a stand like the one Paul took. This isn't a formula to follow. You don't write this down and carry it around with you just in case you run into a demon. In Acts 19, seven would–be exorcists tried that and the demons beat them within an inch of their lives. In our human outlook, we'd like to take hold of the power of God and use it at our discretion, but that's not the way He works.

So for many days, Paul wondered what to do with this woman loudly nipping at their heels. Finally the Lord spoke to Paul who quickly addressed the demon who had taken hold of this woman's life.

In his last letter, Paul wrote to Timothy about doing battle with the devil. "In humility correcting those who are in opposition, if God perhaps will grant them repentance, so that they may know the truth, and that they may come to their senses and escape the snare of the devil, having been taken captive by him to do his will" (2 Timothy 2:25-26). Paul saw those lost in the world as being ensnared by the devil against their own will. "Timothy," he said, "just instruct them in meekness. Who knows what God might do as His Word goes out!"

To the Corinthians, he wrote, "But even if our gospel is veiled, it is veiled to those who are perishing, whose minds the god of this age has blinded, who do not believe, lest the light of the gospel of the glory of Christ, who is the image of God, should shine on them." (2 Corinthians 4:3, 4). Paul's understanding was that Satan blinds peoples' spiritual eyes, perverts judgment, confuses thoughts, and twists the truth. If allowed by God, he will possess the lives of those who don't believe. They are fair game; they live in his house and play by his rules.

At the same time, I think it explains why normal people who react normally to most events will act well out of character in anger or bitterness when the topic of a personal relationship with Jesus comes up. But keep sharing because you never know when God will open their eyes to the truth. That is why I believe that if you are going to share, you ought to pray specifically for the lost that God would bind the enemy.  In Mark 3:27 Jesus tells us that no man can enter a strong man's house and spoil his goods unless he first bind the strong man. Even when Satan has a hold on someone's life, if the Lord binds the work of the enemy, his heart will be open and he'll be able to receive. So pray in Jesus' name. That's where the battle is won. The Lord let Paul speak and the demon came out that same hour. It didn't take five days of prayer and toil, but a few seconds of God's work through the life of His saint! It took the name of Jesus.

*But when her masters saw that their hope of profit was gone, they seized Paul and Silas and dragged them into the marketplace to the authorities. And they brought them to the magistrates, and said, "These men, being Jews, exceedingly trouble our city; and they teach cus-*

*toms which are not lawful for us, being Romans, to receive or observe."*

*—Acts 16:19-21*

Like many businesses today that profit from lust and vice and the misery of others, this business had as well – up to now that is. Rather than rejoicing in this girl's deliverance, there was weeping over a loss of income. In response, they drag Paul and the boys to court, which was held in the open marketplace. The charge was that they were teaching things subversive to the government. Roman law did, in fact, forbid the teaching of religions other than those authorized by the state but since the Romans believed in a zillion gods, that usually wasn't an issue. The real reason this girl's masters' hauled Paul and his team into court wasn't political at all. It was personal. They'd lost their income. But they made it a Jewish/Roman conflict and even accused Paul and Silas of inciting riots. Luke was a Gentile and Timothy, being half Jewish and half Greek, probably looked like a Gentile. Perhaps that's why they were left alone.

*Then the multitude rose up together against them; and the magistrates tore off their clothes and commanded them to be beaten with rods. And when they had laid many stripes on them, they threw them into prison, commanding the jailer to keep them securely. Having received such a charge, he put them into the inner prison and fastened their feet in the stocks.*

*—Acts 16:22-24*

Facing false charges and without a hearing and before an emotional crowd, Paul and Silas are stripped naked and publicly flogged. I have to believe Silas at this point might have been saying to Paul under his breath, "I thought you said you had a vision. Wait until I get my hands on you. You had better hope we don't live through this, pal!"

Jewish law dictated that lawbreakers receive 40 lashes minus 1 for mercy. So they stopped at 39. Romans didn't have any rule like that. Mercy was a foreign concept to them. They just whipped you until they wanted to stop. Bruised and bloody, Paul and Silas were thrown with their feet in stocks into a maximum-security prison cell, which consisted of a hole in the ground with a cover over it.

I think at this point even Paul thought things had gone dramatically wrong. Sure the woman from Lydia and her family and household had been saved. And the Lord had delivered the slave girl. But what in the world was the rest of this all about? It is interesting to me that when we believe God has called us to something, we get so excited when things go well. Yet the moment we run into times of "reversals" in the Lord, times when we're following Him but everything seems to go wrong, that joy quickly escapes us. We want to say, "Wait a minute. This isn't right. God, I've been faithful, now You hold up Your end of the bargain. I got on a boat, sailed over here, talked to women at the river, and dealt with this crazy woman. I've been as faithful as I know how to be and then here You are letting me get beat up. If this is the God of love, I quit!"

And with much the same rationale, we do quit. Where? For one, in our marriages! "God brought us together, would you do the wedding at the church?" the starry-eyed couple asks. A year later, one of them is saying, "I quit." "What are you quitting for?" I ask. "Things are hard. I never expected these kinds of difficulties. God is not blessing!"

You also see people quitting in ministry – people who believe God has called them to start a church and, six months later, they're gone. Or they go to the mission field and quit. Why? I have to believe they quit because when things got hard they questioned whether they had heard the Lord correctly in the first place. Consider Paul and Silas. Things weren't going especially well for them but not one time do we read of them complaining or threatening to quit! They took it in stride, assuming the Lord had other plans.

How do we handle "reversals" in the Lord? After all, serving the Lord isn't always easy. Sometimes it's quite hard. Other times it almost seems impossible! Things don't always go so well or turn out so good. In fact, things can even turn downright rotten before our eyes. Has the Lord failed? Hardly! "I want an explanation," we say. But no explanation comes. "I hate this," we say. "Tough," He says. "Hang in there. Trust Me. I'm doing a good work."

I'm thinking right about now John Mark was thrilled that he decided to join his uncle and travel to Cyprus! Paul and Silas, however, knew God was at work even here in the fire. It was *Onward Christian Soldiers* for these guys as they found themselves beaten, shackled, and bleeding – but right in line with God's plans.

*But at midnight Paul and Silas were praying and sing-ing hymns to God, and the prisoners were listening to them.*

*—Acts 16:25*

In Greek, this reads "they prayed by giving praise in song." Paul and Silas weren't asking God to get them out of jail – which I would have had high on my prayer list if I were them! They weren't asking God to get even with the persecu-tors or the prosecutors or the wicked folks outside – which would have been even higher on my list of priorities. They weren't looking for vengeance; they weren't looking for deliv-erance; they weren't even arguing with God about why He had let something so ugly happen when they had been so faithful. They were just worshipping in the middle of the night.

What an awesome picture of a life lived in the peace and rest that God has for each one of us. I can just hear Silas say-ing, "Hey, Paul, are you OK?" and Paul saying, "Just breath-ing hurts, but, yeah, I'm alright. Hey, Silas, do you know the words to '*Ain't It Grand To Be A Christian*?' I thought maybe we could sing that one together and then maybe we could do that 'Joy, Joy, Joy' song once we get warmed up." In spite of all they were suffering, they sang praises. Amazing isn't it? And apparently they didn't sing quietly. They sang so loud their fellow prisoners must have wondered about the strange new guys in Cell Block D.

From all the Bible tells us, Paul and Silas weren't too concerned with their condition. I can't imagine they were happy. I've been beat up before and I wasn't happy – and I was able to fight back! They might have had better days, but they still sang. And the only explanation for being able to sing is that you are convinced that God knows what He's doing and that He is right. Only then could you sing at a time like this.

People come in constantly for counseling concerning the mess their lives have become whether it's their own fault or someone else's. Rarely do they come in with joy. More often than not, they come in crying. I think Paul and Silas could have done that. But so sure were they of being in the right place with God that even the bleak circumstances could do little to shake their joy or their peace. That ought to be our testimony as well because, although walking with God isn't always easy, it's always right. If you let God have your life, then whatever comes, you can rest knowing He has control of it.

I am reminded of Peter, sleeping the night before he was to be executed – sleeping so soundly that the angel had to deliver him a good "smite" (that's King James English) just to wake him up (Acts 12:7)! God established the early church using men who sing when they get beat up. How do you stop a work like that? You don't! I can't see myself singing in prison but I want to be able to do that.

❑ Day Five Complete – Date: _______________________________________

Application: ______________________________________________________

_______________________________________________________________

_______________________________________________________________

_______________________________________________________________

# Background
## Day Six

*Suddenly there was a great earthquake, so that the foundations of the prison were shaken; and immediately all the doors were opened and everyone's chains were loosed. And the keeper of the prison, awaking from sleep and seeing the prison doors open, supposing the prisoners had fled, drew his sword and was about to kill himself. But Paul called with a loud voice, saying, "Do yourself no harm, for we are all here."*
*—Acts 16:26-28*

This was certainly a selective God involved earthquake. It moved the foundations but it didn't knock down the walls or collapse the roof. It opened the prison doors and gates, knocked chains off the prisoners' legs and arms, yet no one was hurt. It could only be the Lord! It also woke up the sleeping prison guard who could apparently sleep through the worship but couldn't sleep through this. Waking up to his worst nightmare, he saw the prison doors open and a full prison break on his watch. Knowing that according to Roman law, he would pay with his own life for the escape of any prisoner, he quickly decided he was going to save the state some trouble and kill himself.

But God had a much better plan for this man's life than he had for his own. It is not often that you can bring things so far removed together – a man ready to end his own life and God ready to give him one for eternity. And the plan was already set in motion. In fact, it would seem that the beating and the imprisonment and the selective earthquake were all designed for him to be saved.

At that moment, Paul, no doubt led of the Lord, yells out in the darkness, "Hey, don't hurt yourself. We're all here." Now what kind of a silly prison break is that? Doors open; chains fall off – and no one goes anywhere. It could only be the Lord!

Imagine being Paul and Silas for a moment, realizing you have been stripped naked and beaten badly and thrown in jail unfairly so the soul of this man could be reached. Evangelism can be costly. Sometimes you will have to pay the price to reach others with the Gospel. Is it worth it? Ask the jailer and his family when you get to heaven one day! It could be that due to your faithfulness to stand up for Jesus you have lost a job or contact with your family who no longer wants to speak with you or maybe your neighbor thinks you have gone off the deep end. But the result is that your witness touches another life and they find the Lord. Is it worth it to you? To them? To the Lord? And the cost you paid is nothing compared to what Jesus suffered to give you life!

*Then he called for a light, ran in, and fell down trembling before Paul and Silas. And he brought them out and said, "Sirs, what must I do to be saved?"*
*—Acts 16:29-30*

Seconds earlier this jailer was looking death in the eye and then suddenly realized he wasn't ready. Where would he go or what would happen to him? He wasn't sure what was going on but he knew it had something to do with those singing prisoners. So he fell at their feet, trembling, and asked what he had to do to be saved. That's the question most men ask when they're convicted and facing a meeting with God but the focus is still wrong. What can I do? How can I fix it? You can't, but God can!

The question is very similar to what the rich young ruler asked Jesus in Mark 10:17? Lord, he said, I've done lots of things but what else can I do that I might inherit eternal life? What other hoop can I jump through? What other act can I perform? How much more can I give?

*So they said, "Believe on the Lord Jesus Christ, and you will be saved, you and your household."*
*—Acts 16:31*

Paul's answer then would be his answer today. "Everything you need to do has been done. Jesus has done the work – you just have to believe in Him." Paul doesn't give him any rules to follow. He doesn't qualify salvation by some behavior. He just says, "Look my friend; if you want to be saved, believe on Jesus. Believe who He is and believe what He has done and you will be saved – you, your family, anyone, everyone." The entire Gospel presentation in one succinct sentence!

The word "believe" in the Greek is a word that implies you have enough confidence in something to place your entire weight upon it. That is what Paul told the jailer. "Believe on Jesus in such a way as to place your entire life in His hands."

*Then they spoke the word of the Lord to him and to all who were in his house. And he took them the same hour of the night and washed their stripes. And immediately he and all his family were baptized. Now when he had brought them into his house, he set food before them; and he rejoiced, having believed in God with all his household.*
*—Acts 16:32-34*

True belief brings change. It has to because it brings God the Holy Spirit into residence within the heart. It did to the jailer. He took the boys home, cleansed their wounds, and fed them at his own table. Usually jailers don't think too much of prisoners – that is until God lays hold of their life. At home, the jailer's family listened closely as Paul and Silas laid out the plan of salvation in a more thorough manner. As a result, that same night the jailer was saved and so was his entire family! That night they all followed Jesus in water baptism, declaring their new faith in Christ.

It had been quite a day for Paul and Silas, who were now rejoicing greatly even as their wounds caused them to moan now and again. I can hear Paul saying, "Stop making me laugh so hard. It hurts when I laugh!"

*And when it was day, the magistrates sent the officers, saying, "Let those men go." So the keeper of the prison reported these words to Paul, saying, "The magistrates have sent to let you go. Now therefore depart, and go in peace." But Paul said to them, "They have beaten us openly, uncondemned Romans, and have thrown us into prison. And now do they put us out secretly? No indeed! Let them come themselves and get us out."*
*—Acts 16:35-37*

At the end of this eventful day and night, Paul and Silas apparently had to be taken back to prison. The judges, feeling they had made their point, sent word to release Paul and Silas. "Not so fast" was Paul's response. We've been beaten though we have not been condemned of anything. We haven't had a trial. We've been accused and publicly humiliated. And if all of that isn't bad enough, we are Roman citizens. Now you want us to go away quietly? I don't think so. If you want to come let us out, fine – but bring the TV cameras and newspaper reporters. We want to be heard now!

According to Roman law, every Roman citizen was guaranteed a fair trial. And, even if found guilty, Roman citizens could never be flogged. Beatings were for foreigners, slaves, and captives, but not Romans. To mistreat a Roman citizen was to mess with Rome and bring the wrath of Rome quickly upon your head. Men had been put to death for far lesser crimes. Knowing this, Paul now declares, "We weren't treated fairly" – which leads us to question why he didn't tell his captors he was a Roman citizen at the time he was arrested. At the very least, it would have saved him and Silas a good whipping! From this I learn that even though you have rights, it isn't always God's will that you demand them at each step along the way. Had Paul said, "Hey, I'm a Roman," he would surely have been let go; but the jailer would not have heard the good news of Jesus that night and neither would his family have been reached.

I have to believe the only reason Paul didn't speak up earlier is because God had led him not to. He had waited for the Spirit's leading in dealing with the demon-possessed slave girl and I have to believe he was doing the same thing here. Why, then, did he speak up now? One thing is for sure; it wasn't out of spite because that was not a quality Paul possessed. Neither was it to protect his personal reputation which he more than once declared he would leave with the Lord to justify when He came. It appears that he may have spoken up now so that he could buy some protection time for the new little church that had begun to blossom. If for one minute the town leaders thought that this Roman citizen might decide to go to Rome with charges against them, they might handle these few believers in town with kid gloves for a period of time and let them have their way you know, give them a building permit, let them meet downtown for services!

*And the officers told these words to the magistrates, and they were afraid when they heard that they were Romans. Then they came and pleaded with them and brought them out, and asked them to depart from the city. So they went out of the prison and entered the house of Lydia; and when they had seen the brethren, they encouraged them and departed.*

*—Acts 16:38-40*

Again according to Roman law, a Roman citizen could

never be ejected from his own town or from any other Roman town, for that matter. So, unable to order Paul and Silas out of town, the magistrates had to ask them to kindly leave, please. Paul and Silas would indeed move along but not before enjoying a potluck with the woman from Lydia's house. And I don't doubt that they included the jailer and his family and the once-possessed slave girl as well.

So here in our Acts account we are given the story of the birth of the first work of the Gospel in Europe. A church would grow and Paul would eventually write them the very letter we will be studying together here. Even before Paul reached his next destination – the city of Thessalonica – this newborn Philippian church had sent a runner after him with an offering because, so excited and thankful for the work God had done through him, they wanted to help finance the work in the next town. The Philippian church would be one of the few churches that would continue to support Paul for years to come, even when he would later be imprisoned for his ministry.

For now, Paul heads out of town but Luke stays behind to pastor this young church beginning to fill with Christians from all walks of life – a wealthy businesswoman, a very poor slave girl set free from demons, a middle-class jailer who went to work every day to feed his family. The price for some of them to be saved was high, yet no one was complaining and God was busy in them and soon through them.

It seems to me that at least one of the lessons we ought to learn from the planting of this church is that we, too, are planted in a city that God wants to reach and the message is still the same. Exactly how God wants to reach the people of our town and city and surrounding community or at your workplace, only He knows. But I do know He has a plan and wants to use us. It might cost you personally, physically, emotionally, or financially. Are you willing? The work is great and the laborers are few.

❑ Day Six Complete – Date: _______________________________________

Application: _______________________________________________

# Philippians One

# Philippians 1:1-2
# Day Seven

The Book of Philippians is the first of four letters written by Paul from jail in Rome – Colossians, Ephesians, and Philemon being the other three. Paul had been in jail for several years in Caesarea before being shipped to Rome where he would wait several more years to give his defense before Nero, whose verdict would determine not only whether he lived or died but the immediate future of Christianity in every Roman colony and territory. Yet we shall learn that even in this precarious situation, Paul finds joy in the midst of circumstance, a joy based on his fellowship with other saints. For although he was locked up alone, he saw himself as a part of the body of believers and for him nothing could be better than knowing that they loved him, supported him, and stood with him. The topic of the first 11 verses of chapter 1 is just that: fellowship.

While people may use the word fellowship to speak of playing a round of golf with some friends or eating at a meal with some co-workers, the word *koinonia* in Greek speaks specifically of that which we hold in common and as such is used in the Bible with a far deeper meaning than having coffee and pie at a local restaurant. First and foremost, Biblical fellowship or koinonia is basically the commonness that we as Christians possess due to the fact that we all hope in faith, due to the blood that Jesus has shed for our sins. And that hope keeps us together; it is the thing that binds us. Some of us come from very wealthy homes, others from very poor families. Some were very oppressed growing up; others found their lives to be easy. But the thing that holds us together is our common faith that Jesus is the door to life. It is He and our hope in Him that produces true fellowship. We are in the same boat, headed for the same place, and hanging on to the same Lord. That makes us one.

Paul spends the first 11 verses here specifically looking at the joy that comes from the strength of having a like outlook on these things and knowing that you are not in it by yourself when your hope in Him brings difficulty from the world around us. Someone once said to me, "I don't have to go to church to be a Christian." And my answer to them was, "You're right. But to stay strong as a believer and to please God you should go to church because it is His will and it is going to be impossible to sustain yourself on your own. That is why God has given to us the body, you need them as much as they need you."

*Paul and Timothy, bondservants of Jesus Christ, To all the saints in Christ Jesus who are in Philippi, with the bishops and deacons: Grace to you and peace from God our Father and the Lord Jesus Christ.*
*—Philippians 1:1-2*

In the first century, the signature on a letter customarily went at the beginning rather than at the end of a letter. We know Paul wrote this letter because it says so right here at the beginning. If you were in the Philippi church, you would have been pretty excited to receive this letter, especially if you were a jailor, a woman from Lydia, or a poor demon-possessed girl who had been delivered nearly a decade earlier.

As for Timothy, he had been with Paul in Philippi. A half-Jew, half-Gentile, all believer in Christ, Timothy started off doing the work of arranging meetings, booking hotel reservations and carrying the suitcases before becoming pastor in Ephesus. Faithful in the little things, God continued to give him much.

Paul describes himself here as a bondservant of Jesus Christ. In many of the letters he will write, you will find him referring to himself as an apostle by the will of God because at some point in those letters, he has to assert his authority that God gave him as an apostle. You won't, however, find that in this letter, his two letters to the Thessalonians, or his letter to Philemon, because he wrote to them as friends and to churches that were doing well. There was not any doctrinal error in them that he needed to correct as he would, for example, to the Galatians. He didn't need to challenge the immorality that had crept into the church like he would have to with the Corinthians. No, this is a letter from a friend to his friends in the church at Philippi.

The word "bondservant" in Greek is *doulos*, which Paul uses 30-plus times in his epistles. More than just a slave, a *doulos* was someone who had become a slave by choice! The practice came from the Old Testament, where, according to the Law, a slave on the seventh year was allowed to go free. In the Year of Jubilee, the 50th year, all slaves were set free. But if a slave enjoyed his master's house and loved his family, he might choose to become a slave to him for life by choice. His owner would then put a gold earring in his ear, signifying the choice he had made. Paul as a believer and servant of Jesus by choice uses that word to describe himself, as do other saints in the Bible. So we have given ourselves entirely to the Lord and put ourselves at His disposal. Writing to the Philippians from jail, Paul says, "I am a slave by choice to Jesus. My will has been enslaved to the Master; my heart is engaged; my mind is His."

The question could really be asked: "Whose slave are you?," because we are all serving someone or something. You are either a slave to your lust, to the world, to Jesus, or to the devil. Bob Dylan had it right when he sang, "You gotta serve somebody." Paul and Timothy were *douloi*, bondservants of Jesus.

To whom were they writing? To all of the saints in Christ Jesus at Philippi. I like the word "saint." It means to be separated, to be made holy, to be devoted to a single use. In the New Testament, a saint is someone who has given his life to Jesus and, because of that, by faith, has been placed into the family of God. God sees only two classes of people: sinners and saints. There is no third class distinction, such as someone who has yet to decide. There isn't even a "super saint" category. There are just sinners and saints. And, by His definition, saints are sinners who have discovered God's grace in His Son and have been saved.

Like the saints at Philippi, we too are in Christ Jesus. When God looks at you, He doesn't see sin – He sees Jesus. You are cleansed, washed, and whole. And part of the challenge of our Christian walks is to live our lives as His people separated for Him and reflecting His love and mercy and grace in all we do. Saints indeed!

Paul writes to all the saints in Christ, along with the bishops and deacons. When Paul was in Philippi 10 years earlier, there was no need for any church government, no need for a bishop or a deacon. There were just a handful of believers, all about the same age in the Lord. The fact that they now had bishops and deacons meant the church had grown in Paul's absence. The Greek word for bishop can either be *episkopos* – a word that speaks of shepherding or overseeing the flock – or *presbuteros* – which means elder. The terms are interchangeable and speak of elders or overseers, those who are pastoring or shepherding the church, who are responsible for the spiritual well being of the flock.

The word "deacon" on the other hand is *diakonos* and is usually translated "servant." When a church begins to grow, so does its need for organizational structure. Fortunately, in the Bible, the ecclesiastical organization, the church structure, doesn't grow very large or very convoluted. There are deacons and elders, and that's it. Of course there are prophets and pastors and overseers, but they are still deacons or elders. Anything beyond that is man's way of developing hierarchy. Even when the church was adding three to five thousand people a day, we never see anything in Scripture beyond deacons and elders. Elders are responsible for the spiritual well being of the church. Deacons are responsible for the temporal needs of the church – an usher, a person in charge of food ministry, someone who cleans up the fellowship hall, etc.

You might remember back in Acts 6 when the church began to grow very rapidly, the apostles came to the church in Jerusalem and said, "We can study, pray, and teach, but we need help taking food to the widows who need to be properly cared for." Seven men were chosen. One of them was Stephen, who came up through the ranks as a deacon and eventually became the first martyr of the church. In 1 Timothy 3 and Titus 1, you find lists Paul sends to both Timothy and Titus regarding the qualifications they must look for as they sought to develop and choose deacons and elders in the local fellowships.

"Grace to you and peace from God our Father and from the Lord Jesus Christ," Paul writes to the Philippians, blessing them with what has come to be known as the traditional Pauline blessing found also in his letters to the Romans, Corinthians, Galatians, and Ephesians. God's grace brings God's peace to every life that looks to Jesus.

❑ Day Seven Complete – Date: _______________________________________

Application: _______________________________________________________

_______________________________________________________

_______________________________________________________

# Philippians 1:3-6
# Day Eight

*I thank my God upon every remembrance of you, always in every prayer of mine making request for you all with joy, for your fellowship in the gospel from the first day until now, being confident of this very thing, that He who has begun a good work in you will complete it until the day of Jesus Christ;*

*—Philippians 1:3-6*

Sitting on death row for a crime he did not commit and not yet knowing the verdict that would be handed down, how does Paul have any joy at all? He says, "I thank God every time I think about you guys." The thought of the Philippian church brought Paul great joy. It seems remarkable to me that Paul would think about them at all at this point, because when circumstances get rough, we usually think only about ourselves.

"How you doing?" someone asks us.

"Oh, my life is falling apart," we say.

"What's going on?"

"Well, it's the job; the wheel fell off the car; the house was blown over by a hurricane. I'm telling you I have had a week you wouldn't believe!"

Especially when life becomes difficult, we turn to tunnel vision and see things only as they pertain to the circumstances through which we suffer. Not Paul. He had others on his mind. "Bless you, saints," he writes. "I thank God every time I think about you." For Paul, every thought of the Philippians – the fellowship he had with them, the unity they had in Christ – brought him tremendous joy despite where he was and what he was going through.

Now, let me ask you something: to whom would you write a letter, saying, "Every time I think about you, I thank the Lord. Every thought of you fills me with joy?" Who would make that list? And maybe a harder question: on whose list would you be? It was the joy of fellowship that sustained Paul in the midst of difficult circumstances. It was a joy to recall what God had done with the Philippian church and how God had brought them together.

That's really the way fellowship should work for us. "You're having a bad week? That's all right, man. Wednesday is coming. We're going to church. We're hanging around with the saints. I can't wait! I need fellowship like an engine needs gas." I know you can't convince everyone of this – especially those who show up twice a month whether they need it or not – but there is more to fellowship than that, isn't there? "I thank God upon every remembrance of you," Paul said, "so much so that in every prayer of mine for you I make requests with joy. Alright, Lord, here I am, praying for my favorite church again." It seems from his letters that Paul had quite a few favorite churches.

Paul did not pray fitfully or intermittently or sporadically, but always. Paul, if nothing else, was a man of great joy because he had learned how to pray well. "Without ceasing I make mention of you always in my prayers," he said to the Romans (1:9). "I thank my God always concerning you," he wrote to the Corinthians (1 Corinthians 1:4). "[I] do not cease to give thanks for you," he told the Ephesians (1:16). "[I am] praying always for you," he said to encourage the Colossians (1:3). "[I] am making mention of you in [my] prayers," he wrote in his first letter to the Thessalonians (1:2) and "[I] thank God always for you," in his second letter to them (1:3). "I remember you in my prayers day and night," he told Timothy (2 Timothy 1:3). "[I am] making mention of you always in my prayers," he declared to Philemon (4). Wow!

Satan may have thought he had won a great battle when he was permitted by God to put Paul in jail. He might have thought he had kept Paul from doing what was most dear to him, traveling like a man possessed around the world to dangerous places to preach the Gospel. But it seems to me, at least from what you can gather from his letters, he may have actually made it worse on himself by locking Paul up because Paul now had nothing to do but pray. And he seemed to get a lot of praying done and a lot done by praying.

"I always pray for you," he said to the Philippians. Then he said, "I make request for you." The word "request," *deesis* in Greek, speaks of a specific petition. Paul was praying specifically for the Philippian church, not just a general "bless them, Lord." When he prayed for peace, maybe it was for peace with the Romans. We'll read about a couple of women at the end of this book who had been fighting with each other, so maybe he was praying that the Lord would bring peace to them. Whatever the case, Paul's prayers were specific and he was able to offer them with great joy.

Paul didn't pray for everyone that way. To the Corinthians, he said, "For out of much affliction and anguish of heart I wrote to you, with many tears, not that you should be grieved, but that you might know the love which I have so abundantly for you." (2 Corinthians 2:4). It wasn't always happy prayers, but for the Philippians it was. The Philippians were people Paul could find great joy with even in the midst of very difficult circumstances. I believe that should always be the result of the church gathering together – not that we'll always get along or always agree. But there ought to be unity that brings joy into our lives. Our attitude should be, "I can't wait to go and be with the saints in Christ," and thanking God for all that He is doing with great joy.

According to verse 5, Paul was thankful for the fellowship he had with them since day one when the first saint was born again in Christ. The Philippians had stood by Paul since the very beginning of the establishment of their church. They had done what Jonathan had done for David: "strengthened his hand in God" (1 Samuel 23:16). They had always been there for Paul. They had always let him know that they were with him and that he could count on them. From a practical standpoint, a lot of their support was financial. Paul had left and had headed into other places in Europe, but before he had even arrived in the next town, there was already an emissary there from Philippi, saying, "Here, Paul. We know you are probably going to run out of cash before you get home. Let us help you preach the Gospel in this city as well."

The Philippians had helped Paul often and Paul had received it with thanksgiving. He would write in 2 Corinthians 8 how it had been this church who had abounded again and again, willing to give to him and to the work that God had given him to do. They stood with Paul every step of the way. Even when he was 1000 miles away and had been in jail four years, the Philippians hadn't forgotten about Paul. They were with him in fellowship in the Gospel and he knew it. So when he was down, this people and their love filled his heart with joy.

When we read through the Bible, it's easy to forget that Paul was a man. As James wrote of Elijah, Paul was also subject to like passions as we are. He struggled. He didn't have steel nerves. He wasn't free from temptation. And he certainly wasn't free from doubt or discouragement. A couple of times the Lord met him face to face to tell him everything would be all right. In Corinth, he was close to quitting entirely when the Lord came to convince him otherwise. In jail in Jerusalem, he wanted to just give up, figuring he would never get a chance to really get through to the Jews. But God came to him then as well, saying, "Look, Paul, you have been faithful here and now I am going to send you to Rome. Don't worry – this is all going to work out."

Everyone needs encouragement sometimes. But people don't just come up and start asking about your life. Fellowship comes when you give of yourself, get involved, and make yourself available. People ask me why it is that no one in the church ever recognizes them or comes to talk to them. "Do you ever talk to anyone?" I ask. "No, we like to get out early before the traffic starts up in the parking lot," they say. "Well, that is probably why you have so few friends," I say.

The Bible says a man who has friends must be friendly himself (Proverbs 18:24). If you want the most out of your fellowship with the saints, you have to make yourself available. To be honest with you, I'm awful at this. I'm not good at visiting, fellowship, or calling. I don't like it. My tendency is to go home and reach for the TV remote. But I know I need more than that. Joy comes when you know people are with you in the work God has set before you. We are in this thing together, aren't we? God has brought us together here for a work in the community that hopefully will go well beyond us. Paul had such great joy even in terrible circumstances because he had a family that he could turn to. From the very first day, they had been with him. And I don't doubt that Paul, even under house arrest, had a smile on his face thinking about all of those faithful friends who had committed themselves to him and to the work of God.

If you read through the Book of Acts and through the Epistles, you will find that those from Philippi came to Paul in Thessalonica and again in Berea. They showed up in Athens and again in Corinth. And now, as Paul is in his second year in lock-up in Rome, they show up yet again, "Hi, Paul. Philippi at your service. Got a little rent money for you. It's going to be all right. We're going to pray; we're going to bless God." From the first day, nobody from here had given up on Paul. It had been 10 years of faithfulness, together in ministry.

No wonder Paul was confident that He who had begun a good work in them would continue it. *Epiteleo* is the Greek word that means, "to make complete."

When he left Philippi, there may have been six families who had come to meet together. Less than 10 years later, they have many saints and the need for bishops and deacons.

There was plenty of outward proof that they were truly saved and Paul knew when God began a work, He would finish it. I like that. God will never leave or forsake us. What comfort that brings me. If I have to keep myself saved, I'm a dead man. I can't save myself and I can't keep myself. I just stick around where God is and He will keep me. And that was Paul's assurance about this church. They were going to make it because God had begun a work and what God begins, He finishes.

For me, that removes undue pressure from my life each day. Maybe you didn't have this experience, but for the first two years that I was a Christian, I thought I needed to get re-saved about every four or five days. Someone would give an altar call and I'd go forward just to be sure I was saved.

Finally, one pastor spoke up and said to me: "Weren't you up here about a month ago?"

"Yes," I said. "That was me, but that was a whole month ago." So he sat me down and said, "You know, if God begins a work in you, you're saved. You need to have daily fellowship and ask God's forgiveness, but you're saved. Past tense. Your name is written in Heaven. You've got a place to go." Then he taught me this verse.

It is encouraging to know that if God begins a work, He'll finish it. The Lord doesn't lose sight of people even if we have. He won't lose track of them even if we do. They will make it all the way. We might fail people but God won't. In His prayer for the church right before He gave His life for us, Jesus prayed, "While I was with them in the world, I kept them in Your name. Those whom You gave Me I have kept; and none of them is lost except the son of perdition, that the Scripture might be fulfilled." (John 17:12). That's us, isn't it? I talk to people in counseling sometimes who worry about losing their salvation. But that will happen only if God falls off His throne. If He can securely sit there, we'll be all right. If He hangs on, I'll be OK because I'm hanging on to Him. My hope is not that I will hang in there and be faithful. My hope is that He is faithful.

At the end of his life, Paul will say to Timothy, "I know in whom I have believed and am persuaded (a word that speaks of great confidence) that He is able to keep what I have committed to Him until that Day." (2 Timothy 1:12). Talking about the fruit of his ministry, Paul says, "I know that what God did, God can keep. God will work and who shall stop Him?" And it was part of Paul's joy. To the Philippians, he said, "I thank God every time I think about you and am confident that God is going to finish the work He began in you." That applies to you as well if you are in Christ today!

❑ Day Eight Complete – Date: _______________________________________

Application: _________________________________________________

_________________________________________________________________

_________________________________________________________________

_________________________________________________________________

# Day Nine

# Philippians 1:7-11
## Day Nine

*...just as it is right for me to think this of you all, because I have you in my heart, inasmuch as both in my chains and in the defense and confirmation of the gospel, you all are partakers with me of grace. For God is my witness, how greatly I long for you all with the affection of Jesus Christ.*

*—Philippians 1:7-8*

Not only did Paul have the Philippian church on his mind – he had them in his heart as well. Paul genuinely loved these saints. I think sometimes we say we love people but we really don't like them very much. "I have you on my nerves" comes closer to the truth! But not Paul. The Philippian church had moved his heart. They had stuck with him even when his imprisonment and challenges to the Roman government might put them all in a bad light. They were willing to pay the price. Although we can read through it quickly here, it was no small thing to proclaim a kingdom and a God apart from Caesar in first-century Rome. That was like Russian roulette. You had better be sure God was speaking to you because you could very well end up dead. Yet for over nine years, this church had said to Paul, "We're with you, man. Jesus is Lord and we support you, tell everyone about Him!"

You could liken this to hiding the Jews during World War II. It was a tremendous risk to stand with Paul. After all, this guy proclaiming another God was a troublemaker in the eyes of Rome. But Paul said the Philippian church had been partakers' with him both in his bonds and in the defense and confirmation of the Gospel. In other words, they'd been with him through thick and thin. Misfortune and persecution hadn't weeded them out.

The word "defense" is the word from which we get "apologetics" and it means to make a series of statements, one based upon another, to establish one's viewpoint. The word "confirmation" is a legal term, meaning "unconditional guarantee." Paul had made a defense of the Gospel doctrinally and had told the people what Jesus would do, as well as what He had promised for all eternity. Paul brought the defense of the truth and also the promises of God for eternal life. That same motivation that allowed him to risk life and limb gave the Philippians the desire to stand with him. Now, lest you think this would go unnoticed in a little Roman colony like Philippi, remember, these cities were run by Roman ex-soldiers who answered to Rome and oversaw that territory in exchange for governmental favor like paying no taxes. Nero's decision concerning Paul would have a tremendous impact on the church here in Philippi and in many other cities where Roman law would be uniformly applied.

"How greatly I long for you all with affection" literally translates to "I feel it in my gut." Remember the first time you fell in love – or thought you had – how your gut hurt when that special someone hadn't called? Paul says, "I know I can't prove this is how I feel about you – but God is my witness." I don't doubt when Epaphroditus showed up with news from Philippi that a wave of nostalgia washed over Paul's soul, causing in him a desire to be with them. It brought it all back to him!

*And this I pray, that your love may abound still more and more in knowledge and all discernment, that you may approve the things that are excellent, that you may be sincere and without offense till the day of Christ, being filled with the fruits of righteousness which are by Jesus Christ, to the glory and praise of God.*
                              *—Philippians 1:9-11*

As Paul prays for his friends, we now gain insight into some of the things he specifically prayed about. In the Old Testament, the high priest wore an ephod – kind of an odd-looking breastplate that covered his chest and was tied up in the back. In it were 12 different stones representing the 12 tribes of Israel. The point was that whenever he went before the Lord, he brought God's people with him, carrying them on his heart. In that manner, Paul brings the love he has for them to prayer. And his prayer is simple: that their love might abound more and more.

The word love is *agape*, the love that 1 Corinthians 13 defines. *Agape* is a Greek word you don't find used much before the establishment of the church. It's the love God introduced to the world through His Son. It's defined, as a love that denies itself completely and seeks only the best will of another. You can't generate this kind of love on your own because sin won't allow it. But God can put this love in you so that it doesn't matter what you get as long as someone else is blessed. It is best exemplified by Jesus coming for a sinful world, to die in their place, to forgive their sin, and to provide anyone who calls upon His name a way out of sin and death to life eternal. Paul says, "I am praying that the *agape* God has planted in your hearts will continue to grow until it produces even more fruit, until it reaches even more folks, and touches even more lives."

Paul adds the word "abound" and then the words "in knowledge and all discernment" because God's unlimited love has limits. We are called to love all men but not what all men do. Love is to be held out to all, but not gullibly so, not at the sacrifice of truth. Sometimes real love dictates confrontation. If you truly love your kids, you're not going to indulge their every whim. "Honey, I love you but no more ice cream because it will make you sick." So Paul said, "I'm praying that your love will continue to grow as it has towards me and that it will grow in knowledge and in discernment or judgment. No one will ever love us like God loves us, but even God will never love us in a way that violates His holiness or conflicts with His righteousness. He still makes demands upon us in His love.

The word "knowledge" is the Greek word *epignosis*, which speaks of a knowledge that comes by experience. In other words, "I know this is better than that, so, in love, I'm going to choose the best." The word "discernment" is the Greek word for perception or sense. "I'm praying that your love will continue to grow but that you will apply it with good sense and with sound wisdom, having the ability to discern right from wrong, that your love will be able to function in the sense of causing the greatest good."

Sometimes we find love without discernment in very eager, enthusiastic people and it can do more harm than good. For example, if someone is unwilling to work and we give him money, rather than telling him to go to work or he will not eat. In the process, we prop up his unwillingness to be responsible and so we do more harm than good in the name of love. If you love him, call for him to be responsible in his behavior. He might learn from you that he needs to be working, which will really help him. That's discernment. That's love with knowledge. So Paul's prayer for the Philippians was that God would open their eyes so that, as a loving church who had done so much, they would continue to have opportunity to serve and to serve with the love God had given them in a way that would bring great fruit.

True love matures. If you have children, when they are very young, they truly believe anything on four legs is a "bow-wow." But as they grow older, they realize that's not a "bow-wow," it's a cat or a pony or a cow. To a young child everything with four wheels is a car. But I guarantee if you talk to your 16-year-old son, he knows the difference. "Dad, that's not a car. This is a car." He matured. He knows the difference. He talks to you about carburetors and engine sizes and miles per hour. It's the same thing as we grow in the Lord. God wants us to walk in His love and to die to ourselves, but it's got to be love with knowledge based on experience and discernment.

As the church grows, we have many people who come looking for handouts. Sometimes they come looking for housing or food, but usually they want money. And you don't want to be cynical, but many of the stories sound the same: "I've lost my wallet." "The check's coming in the mail." "I'll be all together by the first of the month." We used to give money, but even as we did, we wondered if we were really being helpful. Over the years, hopefully you learn something. So now when people come in and want things, I say, "Great. Are you sick? No? Then we're going to put you to work today pulling weeds. And at the end of the day, we'll pay you so you can buy the food you need. In fact, we'll even buy it for you rather than giving you the money." And if they won't work, we just tell them we can't help.

We should be there for anyone wanting to get off the deck, shouldn't we? But giving money to someone who just wants to hustle us and take God's money for beer or wine or something to eat because they spent everything else they had on booze the night before isn't love with knowledge. It's stupidity and foolishness, so we don't do it. It feels like now we love people with a little more knowledge. And there have been folks who have said, "I'll do whatever it takes to get on my feet." We have seen people like that get saved and it is a good thing.

Paul continues in his prayer that the Philippian church might approve things that are excellent. The word "approve" is *dokimazo*. It means to test and find pure. The word "excellent" is *diaphero* meaning "different." In this case that which is good as opposed to that which is not good. Love the sinner but hate the sin; love people of other faiths but don't love their doctrine. May your love grow to extend even further and to have great discrimination so that you love with God's love, a love that truly seeks the best for another.

Paul prays that the saints in Philippi would be sincere and without offense as they awaited the return of the Lord. The word "sincere" means to be tested by sunlight and is sometimes translated "without wax." In the days of Paul, unscrupulous sculptors who cut too deeply and marred a piece of marble would stick wax into the cuts and color them to look as though the piece was perfect. But when put in the sun, the wax would melt, showing the piece to be "insincere." That is often why contracts discovered from the first century had the word "sincere" in them. Paul prays that the love of the Philippian church might be the real deal, the genuine article, without wax, without offense.

Finally, Paul prays that they would be filled with the fruits of righteousness. The word "righteousness" is a big word but it has the simple meaning of "that which pleases God; is right with Him; of which He approves." The question isn't: "Is it good for me; is it to my benefit; will it make me feel good?" No, the only question is, "Is it right with God?" And this is the difference between you as a Christian and the rest of the world. Most people live outwardly good lives. They pay their bills. They don't steal. They are fairly courteous. The difference between the world and its goodness and a Christian and his righteousness is seen in means and motive. The righteousness shown by the Scribes and the Pharisees was unacceptable to the Lord because it was self-righteousness, an outward show but a heart that is wicked. But God sees the heart, which is why He told His disciples that their righteousness must exceed that of the Scribes and the Pharisees if they ever hoped to enter the kingdom of heaven (Matthew 5:20). We can only imagine what the reactions of His disciples were to hearing these outwardly religious zealots did not have what it took. Yet they had yet to learn that true righteousness is doing what God accepts with a heart He sees.

So Paul says to the Philippian church, "I'm praying that your love will abound, but abound with knowledge and with judgment able to approve the things that are excellent. I pray that it will be without wax and without stumbling and that your life might be filled with the fruit that comes from doing what is right in God's eyes: opening your Bible, saying your prayers, putting God first, seeking first the kingdom of God. May your life be lived in such a way that God gets honor and glory so that you can say with Jesus, 'I always do those things that please Him'" (John 8:29).

Paul's opening paragraph to the Philippians made it clear that, even in his circumstance and difficulty, he had great joy in the Lord because he was a part of the fellowship of the saints. He loved them and took interest in their lives. His own life wasn't his concern as long as Jesus and His Word were going out and changing lives.

"You're saved," Paul said to the Philippians. "I am thrilled! If I die now, I'll die happy, knowing God can take care of you. He started a work, and He'll finish it. In the meantime, you bless me every time I think about you. I'm so thankful for your help. I'm so thankful for your fellowship. I'm so thankful we are in this together."

Like Paul, I love being a part of the Body. And I hope you find joy in the saints as well. We're not perfect – far from it. Yet we all need Jesus, who then makes us one.

---

❑ **Day Nine Complete – Date:** _______________________________

Application: _______________________________

_______________________________

_______________________________

_______________________________

# Philippians 1:12-14
## Day Ten

*But I want you to know, brethren, that the things which happened to me have actually turned out for the furtherance of the gospel, so that it has become evident to the whole palace guard, and to all the rest, that my chains are in Christ; and most of the brethren in the Lord, having become confident by my chains, are much more bold to speak the word without fear.*
*—Philippians 1:12-14*

Beginning in verse 12, we see the second part of joy through circumstance as Paul's focus shifts from the fellowship of the saints to the furtherance of the Gospel. Paul had wanted to come to Rome for a long time and why not? It was the most influential and impactful city of the Roman Empire. If you could reach Rome, you could reach everywhere Rome went. On his third missionary journey in Acts 19, Paul had purposed to go to Jerusalem and then to Rome. When he wrote the Romans a letter, he said in chapter 1 he was ready to come to Rome and preach to them. I don't think he ever planned on going there as a prisoner, yet that's how he eventually arrived.

The story of Paul in Jerusalem and what led to his captivity in Rome begins in Acts 21 and takes us to the end of the book in Acts 28. He was arrested in Jerusalem because he was falsely charged by some with desecrating the temple by bringing a Gentile into a forbidden area. The riots that followed led to his arrest and eventual transfer to a Caesarea prison where he was all but forgotten for two years. He was allowed to give his testimony before kings that passed through, but his release was not forthcoming. Finally, and as a last resort, Paul used his Roman citizenship to appeal his case to Caesar, to the Supreme Court, and only then did his case get some movement. As a result, he was literally shipped off to Rome, which is an overstatement to say the least, as it turned out to be a near-death experience including a shipwreck, a three-month layover in Malta, and a poisonous snake attack. You can read this in Acts 21 through 28.

As Paul is writing he has been in prison for over three years, the last year in Rome. He should have been writing best-selling adventure books or, at the very least, letters saying, "You guys have no idea what I've been going through." Instead, he chooses to refer to it all with a very casual "all the things that have happened to me." Period. He doesn't extrapolate; he doesn't go into any more than that because his interest is not what has happened to him – his interest is how what has happened to him has helped accomplish the will of God to get the message of His Son to the lost. To Paul, it didn't matter that he would be in jail four years, with two of them on death row. He was interested in their lives not his own and the reason he could have such joy in these circumstances is that he had a single purpose. "I just want to see the Gospel furthered," he said. "I just want to see the Gospel taken to every place. And if this is the way God chooses to do it, as long as I can see His hand through the circumstances, I don't care what happens to me."

That's it, Paul? That's why your hair is falling out and you have those wrinkles? "Yeah, everything that has happened to me." Paul found joy in the midst of his circumstances. He not only had fellowship with the saints but he was committed singly to the furtherance of the Gospel, and that ought to be our greatest concern as well. I mean, if not for that, we might as well die when we get saved. When we receive the Lord in Jesus' name we ought to just drop dead because we are not getting any closer to heaven than when we get saved. But God leaves us here for the purpose of taking the Good News to others and we have but a precious amount of time to see that accomplished. Since the day Paul found himself on his back and looking into the glorious brightness of God's presence on the Damascus Road, everything else in his life had taken second place to serving Jesus Christ. And because of that single purpose of heart, no circumstance could steal his joy. To him, everything was an opportunity from God to make Himself known.

Imagine how difficult it must have been for Paul to sit still in a jail cell. Some of us would do fine there, because our lifestyles are laid-back and slow. But Paul was constantly on the move with more energy that we can even imagine. He could hardly sit through a meal. His goals were widespread; preach to every creature upon the earth. Yet now in captivity, rather than complaining, he accepts what God is doing in his life and looks to see what God is going to do through it. If he couldn't go, there must be something he could do. So he writes letters, later collectively entitled his prison epistles. He writes, receives visitors, and shares with his captors. God would work from here, which filled Paul with joy!

After telling the Philippian church how much he loved and missed them and how joyful his heart was because of their love for him, Paul assured them: "Look, brethren, I want you to know that everything that has happened to me has turned out for good – the Gospel has gone even further out." I am sure the Philippians were more than a little frustrated that all they had to show for their many years of corporate prayer on behalf of their Number One Son, and the founder of their church, was that he was still in jail. They'd get up every week on Saturday mornings to pray, "Father, deliver Paul this week … all right, next week … all right, next year … all right, before the elections." But Paul just sat in jail and left some people quietly saying: "The Lord isn't answering our prayers. First he was in Jerusalem; then he was in Caesarea; then we hear about how he almost died. Now he is locked up in some house. When is God going to answer our prayer? We are wasting our time."

Maybe the courier who had brought well wishes and financial support and love from the Philippian church expressed to Paul their worries about not seeing any answers to their prayer.

So as he sits down to write a thank-you letter for their support, Paul adds, "Hey, you are looking at this the wrong way. God has been greatly answering your prayers. In fact, everything has been worth it. My whole life is to glorify Jesus and see His Word go out. And I am telling you; it is going out! The Word is getting out, so your prayers are being answered."

"These things have happened to me to the furtherance of the Gospel." The word "furtherance" speaks of progress or advancement. The Gospel was breaking new ground, reaching new lives, and entering new circles, so praise the Lord! That's what Paul thought. Would you think that after nearly four years of waiting in jail? Probably not. Or two days out of work? Probably not. A lot of circumstances can rob us of joy unless we live for God and our purpose is to get His Word out.

Paul said difficult circumstances had provided new areas of ministry. "I want you to know that what has happened to me has resulted in others coming to know the Lord," he said. And his outlook is hardly surprising. After all, it was with great difficulty that he had shown up at Philippi in the first place. He had wanted to go north to Asia but the Holy Spirit kept pushing him west to Europe. So he went west. And the result was joy, both in fellowship and in the fact that God's Word was getting out.

God had used David with a sling and a smooth stone; God would use Paul in chains; and God will use you in your circumstance if you believe that the greatest and most important issue of your life is being a representative of Christ to get His Word to others.

Paul didn't seem to see any restraint in his chains. In fact, in the last letter that Paul writes to Timothy, he says this: "[Because of the Gospel,] for which I suffer trouble as an evildoer, even to the point of chains; but the word of God is not chained. Therefore I endure all things for the sake of the elect, that they also may obtain the salvation which is in Christ Jesus with eternal glory." (2 Timothy 2:9-10). Even years later when he knew the verdict would be death; Paul's views hadn't changed. He doesn't complain, but rejoices in what God is doing through it all. That's the secret to living a joyful life – a life with purpose.

To the Philippians; Paul goes on to say, "My bonds in Christ are known throughout this place as well as in many other places." Being under house arrest, Paul would have been chained 24 hours a day to a Roman soldier. According to historical records, guards were changed every six hours. So for two years, four guys a day listened to Paul pray with people share with people, and talk about what the Lord was doing. And they were required to just sit and listen. So Paul was encouraged that he was handcuffed to a guy that wasn't saved. The soldier was doing his job – and so was Paul.

Also, his trial was the talk of the Roman legal system because its outcome would determine the fate of the sect Rome called "Christians." But it didn't matter to Paul what the outcome would be. The Word was getting out and the rulers in the Roman government were discussing Jesus on Capitol Hill, in Nero's courtroom. And Paul couldn't have been happier. Now, a jail term of this length for something you didn't do would not be worth it to you if your life had other plans besides serving the Lord. This would be a rip-off, a work of the devil, and a tool of Satan. But for Paul, it was fine, which means he was either nuts or very single-minded, focused on what his calling was.

I think many Christians – especially in the West – spend their lives trying to get the goods of God without paying the price. So when we suffer, it is immediate, isn't it? "Oh, woe is ME! I prayed and everything" we say, as if the sun revolves around us rather than around the will of God. Paul had a single mind and he saw his imprisonment as an advantage to get the Gospel out to the hearts in Caesar's palace, so much so that when he finishes this letter he will sign off by writing, "All the saints greet you, but especially those who are of Caesar's household" (4:22). He saw himself as Agent 007, sharing the Gospel from the inside. So he tells the Philippians, "Look, guys, don't be upset that your prayers haven't been answered in the way you'd like. Don't be grieved that you haven't gotten me out through spiritual warfare. I'm doing what God has called me to do and the fruit is piling up to His glory and I couldn't be happier."

Imagine what the old Roman soldiers in charge of running the government in Philippi thought when they heard that their old stomping grounds were now the place where Paul was preaching. By the time Nero turned against the Christians in Rome, Tacitus, one of the early church fathers, recorded that the church in Rome had grown immensely. In just those few years before all hell broke loose against the church, this work that God began through Paul from prison had literally spread throughout the region.

We are less excited by our trials than Paul was because we are preoccupied with more than just the gospel going forth, and maybe that's the problem. We put Jesus in only one compartment of our lives. Our relationship with God takes a couple hours a week, max. He's not my life; He is part of my life. He is not the one I live for; He's only part of what I do. As a result, I am easily disturbed and perturbed when things don't go my way. I am quickly bothered because I don't really live for Jesus. I live for me, and whatever Jesus might do for me. And if He could bless me, that would be really good because I like me.

Yet you will never find joy in the midst of difficult circumstances unless, like Paul, you also see the Lord in charge, and working out these things for His glory, not mine. The Gospel must be as valuable to you as it was to Paul. If, like Paul, you see that your life is intended to be an extension of the life that Jesus lived and that you're not the focus, then you can be a real joyful Christian in this world because God promises to do the work. He promises to use you. He promises to make Himself known through you.

If you add the four people each day that would sit by Paul to watch over him during these two years, you quickly conclude Paul shared in a month with more folks than many of us do in 10 years of walking with Jesus. What a wonderful opportunity for personal evangelism! Paul saw it that way and the results were that Jesus was made known in the palace and beyond. Paul's chains were not only reaching the lost, they were encouraging the saints. And Paul thought it was great. We might have prayed, "Lord, if You get me out of jail, I'll encourage saints every night." Paul never prayed for that. I never once read of him writing, "Lord, get me out of here." He doesn't once ask the Philippians, "Maybe you all could start fasting so I wouldn't have to be in here for so long!" No, the lost were hearing and the saved were pumped up to speak for themselves. Paul instead encouraged the church, "Don't be discouraged. Great things are happening!"

Discouragement is an easy thing to pass along to people but, apparently, so is faith, because Paul's faith, even in jail, encouraged the church in Rome to speak for the Lord more often. The first time I ever went street witnessing was the most terrifying thing I remember doing as a new Christian. We went to Westwood, California, near UCLA, where the movie "The Exorcist" was playing. When "The Exorcist" first came out, they built a window on the theatre to represent the window in the movie through which a priest gets thrown out by the devil. So we made "open window" tracts, which said, "Have you been thrown out of a window yet? Good! God still has a chance with you."

I went with about eight people from our Bible Study group who were really on fire for street witnessing. I handed out about eight tracts the first night because I was nervous someone would ask me a question and I only knew one verse. But going with those people every week helped me because, although they got angry looks, and a few of them got called names, nobody died. That which was so scary was made a lot easier by watching these other folks who had been out there for a long time. They were bold, yet sensitive, and people got saved. Watching them gave me great boldness. Their faith helped me. I would go home and study, and after awhile, I was the one taking groups of young Christians out to the streets to share our faith. It was a good time; a great time of ministering and learning.

I have to believe that as the saints in Rome went to church on Sundays, they said amongst themselves, "If Paul can reach all these people from jail, certainly we can ask God to use us. I mean, he's filling the church here faster than we are and he's locked up!" What an encouragement Paul was! He had infectious enthusiasm, tireless effort, and boldness in bonds. And the church was changed.

❑ Day Ten Complete – Date: _______________________________________

Application: _______________________________________________

___________________________________________________________

___________________________________________________________

___________________________________________________________

# Philippians 1:15-18
## Day Eleven

*Some indeed preach Christ even from envy and strife, and some also from goodwill: The former preach Christ from selfish ambition, not sincerely, supposing to add affliction to my chains; but the latter out of love, knowing that I am appointed for the defense of the gospel. What then? Only that in every way, whether in pretense or in truth, Christ is preached; and in this I rejoice, yes, and will rejoice.*

*—Philippians 1:15-18*

It seems Paul anticipated the response of some: "But what about the discouraging things that are happening?" He responds here, "OK, not everything on the surface is so rosy. There are actually people out there preaching to make me look bad." Some of the responses to Paul's imprisonment had been to bring out the wicked and the selfish that would use him and his situation for their own devices. That is often the case when God begins to use your life and you begin to step out for the Lord. Opposition will doubtless raise its ugly head. Paul says some had good will, *eudokia*, a sincere heart. They were sharing and reaching out with the right motives. But others were preaching driven by envy and strife.

The word "strife" comes from the root word meaning to run for office, to campaign. It speaks of selfish ambition and is hardly a complimentary term. Paul said, "I know there are some people in the city now preaching Jesus because of me who are looking only to promote themselves. They are only out to get what they can get." Paul's desire for people to hear about Jesus provided a platform for others to preach a similar message but for dissimilar reasons – not so people could be saved but so that they themselves could be made wealthy; so that they could be made known; so that they could be found in the limelight.

Unfortunately, that doesn't sound too far removed from our experiences today where we see sincere people who preach the Gospel to see Jesus honored and lives saved followed by those who are in it for personal gain. That is always the case – God begins a work and soon someone enters, seeking to draw others after themselves. When he left Ephesus, Paul said to the Ephesian elders, "For I know this, that after my departure savage wolves will come in among you, not sparing the flock. Also from among yourselves men will rise up, speaking perverse things, to draw away the disciples after themselves." (Acts 20:29-30).

In Paul's day, there was no shortage of people who were out for themselves. The Judaizers and Gnostics were those with a similar message but used it only to acquire a following, an income, or personal success. They were envious of the Church, envious of the work, envious of the size, and envious of the influence. Religious politics, jockeying for self on the back of the true works of God, is not a new problem. It's an old sin and it still happens. It can't help but happen because when God works, the enemy is angry.

There is a great verse found in Romans 14 where Paul declares, "Who are you to judge another's servant? To his own master he stands or falls. Indeed, he will be made to stand, for God is able to make him stand." (Romans 14:4). I am always very careful before speaking ill of another ministry. If it's the Lord's work, He will fix it; if it isn't, He'll shut it down. God has a great way of ruling.

Paul in jail might have said, "Man, if I get out, there will be lawsuits everywhere! I'm going after everybody! I'm writing a tell-all book. I'm getting a radio show. I'm going to expose everything that is wrong with everyone except my doctrine." But what Paul really said was this, "I don't care if the guy wants to preach to line his pockets. Let him answer to God. God will deal with him. He won't get away with it, but the Word is still true and that Word is getting out and I rejoice in that." How could Paul say that? Because His focus was not on Paul, but on Jesus, and so Paul is not worried about the competition. He doesn't complain about those trying to hurt him. He just admits it's happening and finds God's best in it.

"I know they are preaching out of envy," he says. "I know some of them are doing it out of strife. But there are also some good folks out there. Some are preaching Jesus out of love. They want to stand with the truth. As long as the Word of God is getting out, it will do its work and God will deal with those who would use Him." I'd hate to spend my life trying to figure out what someone else is doing wrong. And I don't see Paul exposing their wickedness. He just lets God be God. What an attitude. What a great outlook. We spend our lives running people down – yet Paul's focus isn't people. It's Jesus.

In Mark 9:38-39, John said to Jesus, "Teacher, we saw someone who does not follow us casting out demons in Your name, and we forbade him because he does not follow us." Jesus said, "Do not forbid him, for no one who works a miracle in My name can soon afterward speak evil of Me." In other words, "He is for us. He may not wear his hair the same way or listen to the same music we do. But God is obviously working so leave room for God to work with others."

God can work in liturgical churches that have a lot of rules and incense and chandeliers and choirs that sing in octaves I can't reach with a ladder. It does not appeal to me, but there are people that like that kind of structure. I totally believe that God works in Foursquare and Assembly of God churches where people like the emotion of it all and feel that if they haven't perspired, God hasn't moved. So what about Calvary Chapel? Well, I think Calvary Chapel is a place where most people live. They are fairly normal; they don't mind wearing shorts to church; they like contemporary Christian music; and they talk about God in a way that you can live with. I think if you fish in the biggest pond, you will attract the greatest audience. You want the Word of God and you want the work of the Spirit. You don't want the Word of God without the Spirit moving. And you don't want the Spirit moving without the guidance of God's Word. Just know He is the One who works — Paul rests in that!

In Numbers 11, the Lord told Moses to choose 70 godly men who were known among the tribes and faithful to the people. He was to bring them to the altar where the Lord would anoint them with the same Spirit that was upon Moses. Sixty-eight showed up the next morning while two stayed in their tents. When Joshua told Moses that the two who had not come were prophesying in the Spirit, Moses said, "Are you upset for my sake? I wish every man was moved by God's Spirit. That would be glorious. I'm not jealous; it is God's work." That's the way Paul felt. We stomp down what we don't like and lose sight of our purpose. Do I support every ministry? No. But I am sure that God can take care of His own and those seeking to be used by Him. Paul had a one-track mind: no envy, no contention, no hatred, and no bitterness. He rejoiced in His oversight and His glory.

John Wesley and George Whitefield were two very powerful evangelists who lived in the 18th century. The Lord used both mightily and both led many to Christ. But, doctrinally, they were often at odds with each other. It was hard to put these two men of God in the same room. When a newspaper asked Wesley if he expected to see Whitefield in heaven, he said, "No way!" Sensing he had a story, the reporter asked why. "Because he will be so close to the throne, I won't ever see him from where I am sitting," Wesley answered.

Wesley didn't appreciate Whitefield's doctrine but there wasn't any envy or opposition. Only the cause of Christ mattered. Although Whitefield and Wesley were in the papers for 30 years, you won't find one word of criticism from either of them about the other. They had tremendous difficulty getting along doctrinally, but they had great respect for each other spiritually, and it showed! That is how Paul could say it didn't matter to him if the purpose for sharing the Gospel was good or evil, envy or love, pretense or truth – the Word was getting out. God would take care of the rest.

❏ Day Eleven Complete – Date: _______________________________

Application: _______________________________________________

_______________________________________________

_______________________________________________

_______________________________________________

# Day Twelve

# Philippians 1:19-26
# Day Twelve

*For I know that this will turn out for my deliverance through your prayer and the supply of the Spirit of Jesus Christ, according to my earnest expectation and hope that in nothing I shall be ashamed, but with all boldness, as always, so now also Christ will be magnified in my body, whether by life or by death.*
*—Philippians 1:19-20*

Paul faced a tremendous crisis. He wasn't a 21st century American with an appeals court process available to him. This was first-century Rome. This was an I-don't-like-the-way-you-looked-at-me-yesterday-so-today-you-die ruler in Rome. "Your prayers and God's grace will get me through," said Paul. "I trust they're going to get me out. But I'm only truly concerned with leaving a good example so that whether I live or die, I will have been bold in Jesus' name. The most important issue to me is not being released or exonerated but being sure to leave a witness for others that will bring them to Jesus."

In essence that had been the very topic of Paul's letter to this point: the glory of our Lord! Paul's concern wasn't deliverance from his situation as much not saying or doing anything to bring shame to the name of Jesus. He wanted to be sure the Lord would be glorified in his body, in his life, to the very end. The word "magnified," means in Greek what it does in English: to make large. I want to live in such a way that Jesus is enlarged through my life – that people see Him clearer and better; that He is seen more readily by the way that

I live, that He will be glorified and praised and honored by my response to all of this pressure. To Paul, more important than living or dying was making sure Jesus was glorified in his life. What a great concern!

If we stop to think about that first, we would do things a lot differently, wouldn't we? Most of us are pretty bold when we're in control, but when we are in His hands that sometimes changes. Notice what Paul says in verse 21 …

*For to me, to live is Christ, and to die is gain.*
*—Philippians 1:21*

If that is the case, how can you lose? If I am alive, I live for Jesus; if I die, I am better off, for I then go to be with Him. What if you had to fill in these two blanks? For me: to live is ______ and to die is ______. Would you say the same thing Paul just said?

Balaam was a false prophet who lived his life in defiance of God and tried to use what God had given him for his own benefit, at each turn in utter disobedience. Yet when he considered the believer's life, he declared his secret wish, "Let me die the death of the righteous" (Numbers 23:10). In other words, he wanted to live like hell and die as a saint. But that doesn't work. For the majority of men, people die like they live and whatever went into the blanks will usually stay there. Very few change their minds on their deathbeds. I know of the thief on the cross, but I'd be hard pressed to find six others in the Bible who experienced a true deathbed conversion.

Paul here faced death as he had lived: honoring the Lord. He just wanted to make sure he wasn't going to be compromising his testimony in the process.

*But if I live on in the flesh, this will mean fruit from my labor; yet what I shall choose I cannot tell. For I am hard-pressed between the two, having a desire to depart and be with Christ, which is far better. Never-*

*theless to remain in the flesh is more needful for you.
And being confident of this, I know that I shall remain
and continue with you all for your progress and joy of
faith, that your rejoicing for me may be more abundant
in Jesus Christ by my coming to you again.*

*—Philippians 1:22-26*

"I don't know exactly what is going to happen," said Paul, "but I believe I will probably get out of here, show up on your doorstep, and you will be happier in the Lord than ever. Four years of praying and you will get what you want. It will encourage your faith." Paul was facing the ultimate outcome and, for himself, he couldn't decide whether he would rather live or die. For him, it was far better to leave; yet his ministry would help many others in their walks.

The word "desire" in verse 23, *epithumia* is the word for "lust." It is one of only a few places in the Bible that it is used in a good sense. Usually lust is bad – it's fleshly and sensual. But Paul says, "Whatever I have got going, I lust to be in heaven. That's where my desire lies."

From 2 Corinthians 12, we know that Paul had been to heaven. You might remember that account in Acts as Paul was dragged out of town in Lystra, stoned, and left for dead (Acts 14). He would write to the Corinthians that he wasn't sure if he had left his body or not but he was sure he had gone to the third heaven. "I would like to tell you about it," he said, "but it would be a sin for me to try to put into words what I saw. I couldn't do it justice so I had better not say anything except to tell you that it was really something. And because of the multitude of these visions, God gave me a thorn in my flesh so that I wouldn't be more proud of myself or be more filled with myself than I ought to be."

At this point, Paul might have thought, "I could go there again. How good would that be?!" But the thorn in his flesh kept his feet on the ground.

"Whether I should depart or not I don't know," he

writes. The word "depart" is a military term. It means to break camp, pull up stakes, and take down the tent. The Bible speaks of our bodies being like tents taken down at death when we go to be with Jesus. Paul didn't have any fear about dying and yet he knew that staying would be a benefit for the Church. His thoughts raced back and forth from the harps and halos to the dirt and the dust. Despite all he had suffered to come to Rome, Paul categorized his life very easily: everything that had happened to him had turned out for good. He didn't dwell on the shipwrecks or chains; he just wanted to talk about the Gospel. The Gospel was getting out and the Church was beginning to hit the streets. What a great outlook; what a great joy! A single mind is not overcome by circumstances but sees them as opportunities for the fellowship of the saints and the furtherance of the Gospel.

❏ Day Twelve Complete – Date: _______________________________

Application: _______________________________________________

___________________________________________________________

___________________________________________________________

___________________________________________________________

# Philippians 1:27
# Day Thirteen

*Only let your conduct be worthy of the gospel of Christ, so that whether I come and see you or am absent, I may hear of your affairs, that you stand fast in one spirit, with one mind striving together for the faith of the gospel,*

—*Philippians 1:27*

The word "only" is the Greek word for "whatever." Paul says, "Whatever happens to me, make sure you are living in such a way that brings honor to the Lord as well. I don't know if I am going to live or die; I don't know if I am going to be in jail for a long time – but no matter the outcome of my situation, make sure that you live your lives as good witnesses for Jesus and that you strive together for the faith of the Gospel." After telling the Philippian believers that his suffering was worth it to him as the Gospel was going forth and many were being saved, Paul encourages them to stand up for the things of the Lord as well because doing so is worth the cost, and many lives will find eternal life through Jesus Christ.

The word "conduct" is the Greek word, *politeuomai* meaning citizenship. The Philippian believers had dual citizenship. On the one hand, they were from a Roman colony and, as such, were free Roman citizens. Protected by Roman law, they could have been very proud of their status. On the other hand, Paul tells them they were also citizens of heaven. He will mention it again in Philippians 3:20. Paul was concerned that, in the midst of the suffering they were facing, there were certain people in the church that might at some point quit conducting themselves as citizens of God's Kingdom and seek rather to fit in to their other citizenship again.

In the first century, no one in his right mind would have thought about breaking Roman law. The cost was just too great. In like manner, Paul told the Philippian church that they shouldn't think about backing away from the faith of the Gospel, though the cost might be high for standing up for it. It was a difficult challenge. Imagine living today in a Muslim or Hindu culture and being told to live like a child of God, to honor God's Word and obey it, regardless of what anyone else says; being told to keep up your end of the bargain as a citizen of God's Kingdom and to stick with His ways and His Word regardless of the cost or the outcome.

Had the Roman judgment turned against Paul at this point, the practice of Christianity would have been immediately outlawed, as his case would have had landmark implications. Christians would have been put to death on the spot. Yet not knowing for sure what the outcome of his trial would be, Paul says, "If I die, you live for Jesus and be sure that you live as a citizen of His Kingdom. Don't back away from following Him now. The cost is great but the reward is greater."

The most important asset Christians have in reaching the lost is not a good message skillfully preached but rather steadfast living for Jesus. The consistent life of the believer in the eyes of the world is as good as it gets. It is worth remembering that often the only thing the world knows of the Gospel is what they see of it in your life. Part of the joy Paul experienced in his circumstance came from the realization that if he maintained his relationship with God when things were this contrary, unbelievers would take notice.

The same, of course, is true of us. "Wow, you lost your job and look at you – you're just trusting the Lord. You're weird!" people say. But then they begin to notice your peace. You didn't fall apart; you didn't fly off the handle; you didn't go back to the bottle; and you didn't give up. You waited on

God and He was faithful. In general, everyone is happy when things are going well. What makes you unique as a Christian is that even in the worst of times, you know God is still on the throne. In the worst of times, you know all things still work together for good to those who love Him and are called according to His purpose. The world doesn't know that but they see those truths in you. They think the wheels of life have fallen off, but you know God's in charge and so you can rest with joy. So it was with Paul in jail!

Paul realized that the eyes of the world were upon him as he stood fast in this very difficult time. Yet to him, it wasn't a trial, it was an opportunity. To him, it wasn't difficulty, it was joy. It's like the pastor who had a request from a man in his church for some literature to give to his neighbor who was involved in a cult. The pastor opened the Bible to 2 Corinthians 3:2 and read, "You are our epistle written in our hearts known and read by all men." The pastor then encouraged that man, "Go hang out with your neighbor and you show him what Jesus is like."

When Gandhi was asked what the greatest hindrance to Christian missionary work in India was, he said, "Christians!" Granted, he wasn't pro-Gospel, but it is an interesting comment, especially when Jesus said, "You shall be My witnesses…to the end of the earth" (Acts 1:8). Paul called these Philippian saints to live in such a way that there wouldn't be a difference between their message and their lifestyle. To the Ephesians he would write, "I beseech you to walk worthy of the calling with which you were called" (4:1). To the Colossians, he would say, "That you may walk worthy of the Lord" (1:10). And to the Philippians, he says, "Whether I am absent or whether I get there, all I want to hear is that you stand fast in one spirit." The phrase "stand fast in one spirit" is only one word in Greek, *steko*, and means to persevere.

Throughout the New Testament, the phrase "faith of the Gospel" is a term that denotes and encompasses the entire body of truth of the Gospel: the deity of Christ, the death and resurrection of Jesus, the need to be born again, the coming of the Spirit, the passing from death to life, the mercy through the blood of the Lamb. The faith of the Gospel speaks of the basic truths that God gave the Church. Paul tells the Philippians, "You guys have to stand together to adorn the Gospel of Jesus. And in your stand, be of one mind and of one spirit, striving together for the basic truths of Scripture now more than ever before."

One truth every generation of saints desperately needs to hear is that their calling as God's people is to shine in the world and stand fast for the truth, which the enemy will consistently seek to undermine.

Paul would write to Timothy, "Now the Spirit expressly says that in latter times some will depart from the faith, giving heed to deceiving spirits and doctrines of demons." (1 Timothy 4:1). In chapter 6, he continued, "O Timothy! Guard what was committed to your trust, avoiding the profane [and] idle babblings and contradictions of what is falsely called knowledge" (1 Timothy 6:20). There is too much work to be done for us to be fighting amongst ourselves, especially when the work God has called us to is to present the Gospel in unity with lifestyles that certify the message as true. Satan's work, on the other hand, is to destroy, to divide, to undermine, to rip off, to take away from the faith. What is our first and best witness? It is the love that God placed in our heart by the presence of the Holy Spirit. "By this all will know that you are My disciples, if you have love for one another." Jesus said in John 13:35.

As you read the book of Philippians, don't think for a minute that things were perfect in the church at Philippi. Do you know any church that is perfect? Don't join it – you'll wreck it! In chapter 4, Paul will actually name names of troublemakers in the church. Because of this, Paul wants to focus them again on what they were called to do – to stand together for the sake of the Gospel.

I read a story about a father who had five sons that never got along (which doesn't seem too surprising!). He had the oldest of them break a bamboo cane. He told him to put the two pieces together and break them again, which the son did. Then he told him to put the four pieces together and break them again. Being a big kid, he broke four, broke eight, but could not break 16 pieces. His dad made a quick application, "If you stand together, you'll be strong." That's the way the church ought to be. The church must present a united front for the sake of the Gospel, which is why Paul talks to them about their effort in light of their witness.

The phrase, "striving together," or *sunathleo* in Greek, comes from two words. Sun means "with" – Paul uses it 16 times in this letter alone to put people together – while *athleo* is the word from which we get our English word "athletics." When Paul tells the Philippian church to strive together, he's telling them they need to work together sharing their faith in the same manner athletes on a team do to win. All team sports require team attitudes to win. The difficulty comes when you get a glory hound on the team. Maybe you have been on teams like that – with a guy who always wanted the ball, always took the shot. That can also happen in the church. In his third epistle, John says, Be careful of Diotrephes. He wants to be first in everything (3 John 9).

James and John had come to Jesus with Mom, asking for season tickets in heaven – box seats right next to Jesus. "It won't be like that in My Kingdom," Jesus said. "Whoever desires to become great among you, let him be your servant" (Matthew 20:25-26). Christianity is a team sport. God has risen up a single body, not a bunch of little bodies. And He has brought us together for the sake of being a witness for His Son, who would make the ultimate sacrifice for each of us.

How do I find joy in difficult circumstances living as a Christian in this world? In part, by knowing I am part of a team. Why do I look forward to coming to church? Because I am not nearly as well accepted in the world as I am here, and neither are you. At church, most love Jesus. Because of that I look forward to hanging around with them. It's nice to be in it together. We all sink or swim together. That doesn't mean everybody is called to be a quarterback or that everyone is called to receive the ball. But everybody has the same rules and the same goal. For us, the goal is to bring people to Jesus, to honor the Lord in our fellowship, and not give up the faith of the Gospel when the road becomes difficult. For Jesus is the only hope of salvation for all men.

"Whatever happens to me," Paul says, "you have to stick together in this thing like a team. You've got to persevere with one spirit for the truths God has delivered to you."

❑ Day Thirteen Complete – Date: _______________________________

Application: _____________________________________________

___________________________________________________

___________________________________________________

___________________________________________________

# Philippians 1:28
# Day Fourteen

*...and not in any way terrified by your adversaries, which is to them a proof of perdition, but to you of salvation, and that from God.*

*—Philippians 1:28*

The word "terrified" is the word that means to shy away like a horse from a shadow or something that jumps out in its path, to be spooked or startled. "Don't let the enemy alarm you," says Paul. "Your strength lies in sticking together because you are unified in your faith and in your courage."

Your confidence is an evidence of your sure faith. The word "proof" here means demonstrated proof, a clear sign, and undeniable evidence to the unbeliever that he's not saved but you are. Your confident response to persecution as well as your willingness to stand fast in the Gospel is proof positive that you are saved by God and that the unbeliever is not. You can't have that strength without God's help. You couldn't stand even if God wasn't there to help. You are saved while the unbeliever is on his way to perdition – a word that means utter destruction and is used a couple of times in the Bible to speak of hell itself. Your undaunted courage in the face of circumstance, your perseverance as one spirit, and your striving together with one mind, will prove much, both to you and to the lost, of your relationship with Jesus Christ.

In Psalm 27, David wrote,

*The LORD is my light and my salvation; Whom shall I fear? The LORD is the strength of my life; Of whom shall I be afraid? When the wicked came against me To eat up my flesh, My enemies and foes, They stumbled and fell. Though an army may encamp against me, My heart shall not fear; Though war may rise against me, In this I will be confident. One thing I have desired of the LORD, That will I seek: That I may dwell in the house of the LORD All the days of my life, To behold the beauty of the LORD, And to inquire in His temple. For in the time of trouble He shall hide me in His pavilion; In the secret place of His tabernacle He shall hide me; He shall set me high upon a rock. And now my head shall be lifted up above my enemies all around me; Therefore I will offer sacrifices of joy in His tabernacle; I will sing, yes, I will sing praises to the LORD.*

—Psalm 27:1-6

What a gift that God has touched your life in such a way that your conviction about the truth of His Word gives you so much strength. Even when you suffer, your diligence does not wane. That's a different story than most. Most people's convictions reach only as far as their comfort zone or their pocketbook. "I don't drink on the job, unless you're buying, and then I'll have a double." Often convictions change depending on circumstance.

Paul says clearly, "I don't know what is going to happen, but whatever it is, you have to stick together because it is the faith of the Gospel that will see you through. You don't need to be terrified of your enemies. God is in charge. And knowing this is going to be proof to the world that you have more than they do, that you have a strength beyond yourself, that you know the Lord of all."

Paul writes to the Romans in chapter 8,

*What then shall we say to these things? If God is for us, who can be against us? He who did not spare His own Son, but delivered Him up for us all, how shall He not with Him also freely give us all things? Who shall bring a charge against God's elect? It is God who justifies. Who is he who condemns? It is Christ who died, and furthermore is also risen, who is even at the right hand of God, who also makes intercession for us. Who shall separate us from the love of Christ? Shall tribulation, or distress, or persecution, or famine, or nakedness, or peril, or sword?*

*—Romans 8:31-35*

Who shall separate us from the love of Christ? The answer is, "No one."

An eternal change takes place in my life when I become a Christian. From the moment the Holy Spirit took up residence in my life, I have been unwilling to go backwards. My life was changed. So don't be moved from your determination to live as a Christian by anything your enemy seeks to do. Their opposition to the Gospel is a sure sign to them of their condemnation. But to you it is a sign that God is working. Read Foxe's Book of Martyrs, which records so many examples of those who laid down their lives willingly for the faith. "Deny the Lord and you live," they were told. "I can't," they replied. "God didn't deny me."

❏ **Day Fourteen Complete – Date:** ________________________________

Application: ____________________________________________

_______________________________________________

_______________________________________________

_______________________________________________

# Philippians 1:29-30
# Day Fifteen

*For to you it has been granted on behalf of Christ, not only to believe in Him, but also to suffer for His sake, having the same conflict which you saw in me and now hear is in me.*

*—Philippians 1:29-30*

"It has been given to you," said Paul – not "forced upon you." It is a gift, a privilege, that, not only would you believe in Christ, but that you would suffer for His sake. Yet suffering for suffering's sake is certainly no privilege. To have a hard time because you act the fool is never applauded as good. Peter writes that if you suffer as an evildoer you get what you deserve. But if you suffer for being a Christian, that is something God accepts and blesses (1 Peter 4:15-16).

To be able to enter into the work of God in some small way–even if it costs us something–is a privilege. I don't know if you see it that way, but Paul did. And, because of that, he was joyful in the circumstances he faced.

In Acts 4, you see the church being persecuted for the first time. The apostles were told to never again preach in the name of Jesus, told that the next time they did they would face dire consequences. Yet they ignored the warning and, when they were released, lifted up their voices to God in one accord, saying, "Lord, You are God who has made the heavens, the earth, and the sea. You hear what our enemies are saying. Now give us boldness to go out and speak in Your name" (Acts 4:23-33). In chapter 5, they were re-arrested, beaten, and told, next time, they would die. When they were released, we read that they left being thankful that they were able to suffer shame for Jesus (Acts 5:41). Only a saint who realizes the price the Lord paid to save Him could make such a statement and mean it.

The very words "on behalf of Christ" or "for Jesus' sake" alone should draw our interest. After all, I owe Him so much. He suffered more than anyone and He did so to save you and me! Now Paul turns to say that sometimes it is given to us to suffer on behalf of Christ. Is it worth it? Sure it is. What if, because of my willingness to suffer, someone gets saved? Was it worth it for someone to share with you when you were laughing at them? Of course it was. If they had quit, you might never have come around. But here you are, praising the Lord. When my best friend shared the Lord with me, I said, "Man, you are way too uptight. I see God almost every night" – and offered him a joint. Was being made fun of worth it to him? I'm not sure it was to him that night. But it was to me when I surrendered to Jesus!

Sitting in jail, possibly soon to be killed, Paul is trying to convince a church that is in relatively good shape to quit fighting with each other and to stand together for the sake of the Gospel because it is worth it to live your life for Jesus no matter the circumstance. How long is it worth it? To Paul, it would be worth it until he was dead and standing before the throne of God.

Unfortunately, you and I as Christians often see difficulty, not as a privilege given to us by God to be used for His glory, but as a punishment from God for no apparent reason. We see a lack of faithfulness on God's part to answer our prayer when we have been asking for weeks to get out of our circumstance. "No," says God. And we say, "Why not? It's not fair. How come my friend Bill doesn't face a circumstance like mine?" Yet Paul saw all difficulties as a privilege and a sure sign of his salvation and as an open door to reach many with the Good News of Jesus.

If asked why God would allow suffering in the lives

of His people, Paul would say it is so others might see who Jesus is through the life lived by a citizen of heaven. Why is God silent sometimes when we cry out for deliverance? For the same reason He was silent when Jesus cried out, "My God, why have You forsaken Me?" Why didn't God deliver Jesus right then? Because if He had, you would be lost. Jesus hung silently and, as a result, you were saved. Now you are suffering and the Lord wants to use your suffering as a witness to others of who you are and who your God is.

Paul's sufferings seemed endless. Yet to him, each trial brought him closer to his goal of reaching the lost. He discounted the prison; he discounted the pain; he discounted the persecution; he discounted the years in jail. They were nothing compared to what had been accomplished.

I don't doubt that somewhere along the line, Paul memorized this part of the Sermon on the Mount where Jesus said, "Blessed are those who are persecuted for righteousness' sake, For theirs is the kingdom of heaven. Blessed are you when they revile and persecute you, and say all kinds of evil against you falsely for My sake. Rejoice and be exceedingly glad, for great is your reward in heaven." It is through suffering that the world gets to see who is walking with God and who isn't. Jesus went on to say, "For so they persecuted the prophets who were before you" (Matthew 5:10-12). Unto you (the church) has been given on behalf of Jesus not only to believe in Him (that's the fun part) but also to suffer for His sake (that's the hard part). Yet it's only hard because we don't properly understand that in heaven, the rewards will match the cost and the work of Jesus in bringing people out of darkness to the Light will have been accomplished. God never wastes suffering.

The old saying was: bear the cross, wear the crown. "I don't want to bear the cross, I just want to wear the crown," we reply. But it doesn't work that way. Peter wrote,

*Beloved, do not think it strange concerning the fiery*

*trial which is to try you, as though some strange thing happened to you; but rejoice to the extent that you partake of Christ's sufferings, that when His glory is revealed, you may also be glad with exceeding joy. If you are reproached for the name of Christ, blessed are you, for the Spirit of glory and of God rests upon you. On their part He is blasphemed, but on your part He is glorified.*

—1 Peter 4:12-15

According to Peter, God is glorified by the way we suffer. It's one thing to say, "I love God who has forgiven me," but if I forgive no one, that message is quickly lost. If I say the reason I won the lottery is because God is in charge of my life, that doesn't explain very much. But if I say, "I don't know why I am going through these unexplained challenges, but I know God has a purpose and I am going to rest in Him knowing that," what a witness that is! Paul was a great witness, a man of peace and joy. There are many benefits to suffering. It sure draws you closer to Jesus. I've never seen suffering Christians forget to pray. On the other hand, I have seen all kinds of happy-go-lucky, blessed Christians forget to pray. They devalue prayer in a hurry, but the minute they need something, their knees find the ground really fast.

Not only that, but we are told that suffering now will bring rewards later. Paul said it in Romans 8:18 when he wrote that the sufferings of this present time are not worthy to be compared with the glory which shall be revealed in us. He said it to the Corinthians when he wrote that our light afflictions which are but for a moment will work in us a far more exceeding and eternal weight of glory (2 Corinthians 4:17). God gives us the opportunity to shine in the midst of trials. If we have that single mind, we can have joy even in the worst of circumstances and become a light to people in darkness.

I think that the world's opinion of most Christians is that they are very similar to the world: happy when things go well and unhappy when they don't. Up and down just like everyone else. Therefore, the witness of the church shines its brightest when the chips are down. There is great benefit to the plans and purposes of God in suffering. Never forget that.

When He called Paul, Jesus said, "For I will show him how many things he must suffer for My name's sake" (Acts 9:16). Suffering is part of our calling. It's a gift, though, not a punishment. It's not an angry move on God's part – it's a blessing. "I want to use you," He says, "so you are just going to have to put up with hurting for Me. After all, I hurt for you." But how do we do that? We do it together, striving together with one spirit and one mind.

"You have the same conflict which you have seen to be in me and now hear to be in me," Paul tells the Philippians. If the enemy can get you to think that you are all alone in suffering, you are liable to quit. Paul says, "You are just going through the same thing I did when I was there." When Paul was in Philippi, he was arrested for being used by God to cast a demon out of a slave girl. He brought her back to her senses and returned to her the ability to make right choices. But what did the town leaders say? "Oh, no. We'll have none of that. No healing in this town. You're going to jail – but first we'll beat the tar out of you."

Paul reminds the Philippian church, "You remember what happened to me – and what is still happening to me – and now you are facing it to some extent as well." Satan would like you to think that you are all alone in your suffering and that it will accomplish nothing. That's why Paul points to himself. "Look at me. You saw it when I was there; you hear about it now; and I am writing to tell you God is at work mightily despite what you might conclude." Paul had faced trials like they faced when he was with them; he was still facing them in Rome, some 800 miles away –and the fruit continued to be brought in each day. So he exhorts them to rejoice in circumstance, to view suffering for Jesus' name as a privilege, and to greatly value its worth in God's hands and in God's plans.

When people tell us to cheer up and trust the Lord, our tendency is to think, "Sure that's easy for you to say – you still have a job." Or, "Your wife still lives with you", or "your parents are still talking to you", or "it wasn't your name on that lawsuit; it was mine! How am I supposed to rejoice?" Paul would answer, "Let me tell you about suffering …" You might not accept counsel from someone who has had an easy life, but you've got to listen to Paul. He knows exactly what you're going through. In fact, he wrote the book on it.

Could I, like Paul, be willing to die for my faith? To be honest, I don't know. I trust that if God puts me in that situation, He will give me the strength for it. He promises, "As your days, so shall your strength be" (Deuteronomy 33:25). I lost a wife at 25 to leukemia. I was left to raise two children under 3-years-old. I didn't think I could do that. But I did. Because I am good? No, I would have complained night and day. But God bailed me out. I see people in our Body who have gone through far worse things and made it just fine. Is it because they are strong? No, it's because God gave them the grace for what they needed to do. And He promises to never put us where we would be overwhelmed (1 Corinthians 10:13).

Paul says to the Philippian believers, "You have the same conflict I had." What is the conflict? It is the persecution of the saved by the lost. "I love you guys," Paul says. "I am glad that you love me. All of my suffering has borne great fruit. I hope to get out, but I may die. Either way, I am living for Jesus. If I get to hang around awhile longer, then I get to help you some more. If not, you'll go on without me. But make sure that whatever happens, you are together in this thing."

One of our strengths as the church is that we are together in the world. We are a minority, you know. Most people aren't saved, but you are. So your job is to go out into the world filled with the lost and be a witness. I think the only way we can do that is to do it together. Let's live out our Christian citizenship in such a way that Jesus is honored, that fruit comes from our lives, that we have joy in the midst of circumstance. If you consider those things every time you are about to react to something in your life, your reactions might change. Remember your purpose for being here is so people can see Jesus. What you say and do matters!

What are people reading in your life about Jesus? I hope they see the joy of fellowship, the joy of the furthering of the Gospel, the joy and the privilege of suffering for Jesus. In the world, you will have tribulation, but be of good cheer… Present suffering is nothing compared to what we are going to get as a result. Are you willing to put up with a little? What and who are you living for?

❏ Day Fifteen Complete – Date: _______________________________

Application: _________________________________________

_________________________________________________

_________________________________________________

_________________________________________________

# Philippians Two

# Philippians 2:1-4
# Day Sixteen

Through a long series of events, the first place Paul visited on his second missionary journey to Europe was Philippi. A Gentile woman from Lydia, who had been converted to Judaism, was saved. Eventually her entire family came to the Lord and their home became the meeting place for the church. Then a demon-possessed girl was delivered by the Spirit of God from demons that had possessed her for some time. Finally a jailer and his middle-class family were saved as well – and from this group a church began. Paul wasn't there long before being arrested, beaten, and unfairly imprisoned, all without a trial. He was then asked to leave town. By the time of this writing, nine years or so have passed since that church plant and Paul is in jail in Rome. He has been allowed to present his case and, no doubt, the gospel as well, before Caesar Nero and now waits to hear his fate. Either he will be released having been exonerated from ridiculous trumped up charges or he will be beheaded, having been found guilty of them by this madman in Rome. As he awaits the verdict, Paul receives a visit from a brother in the Lord named Epaphroditus who brings to him a gift, an offering from the Philippian church. It was the initial impetus for Paul writing this letter, to thank them for their ongoing faithfulness and support. But in the process of writing, Paul composes his greatest single treatise on joy that we have.

In chapter 1, he writes about the joy in his heart despite the circumstances he was facing and had faced. In chapter 2, he writes of his joy despite what some people might do to steal it from him. In chapter 3, he writes of his joy in the Lord despite the lack of many things. He closes with chapter 4, writing of his joy that can overcome fear and worry.

If the key verse of chapter 1 is verse 21: "For me to live is Christ, and to die is gain," then the key verse of chapter 2 is found in verse 5: "Let this mind be in you that was also in Christ Jesus." Here in chapter 2, Paul gives us his concern in verse 1, his encouragement in verses 2-4, and then four examples to highlight the principle he establishes in the first four verses. Jesus is, of course, his ultimate example in having joy despite the people he faced. Paul uses himself as the second example of that joy before turning to his longtime protégé, Timothy, beginning in verse 19. Lastly, beginning in verse 25, Epaphroditus will be Paul's fourth example of overwhelming spiritual joy. This is despite how the actions, words, and behaviors of people might steal that joy from you.

Though the Philippian church had an excellent track record of love and had borne great fruit, they still, like every other church, had domestic problems. In the first couple of verses of chapter 3, Paul will reference some false teachers who had entered into the fellowship from without, hoping to turn the hearts of the people away from God and His ways. And in the first few verses of chapter 4, we are told of two ladies within the church who were having a public and protracted feud within the church. We are not told exactly what the problem was but are told that saints in the fellowship were taking sides and the church was left divided. Paul's concern was for them and for the church as a whole because division, strife, and contention are a terrible witness and a breeding ground for the enemy's ways. He saw it as a spiritual issue that wouldn't be resolved by taking one side over the other, by determining who was right and who was wrong, by mandating rules, or by taking a stand with the loudest, meekest, or quietest. It would be resolved only on a personal level because strife comes from pride and self. And the only thing that can change pride and self is a heart that has been turned towards God. That will be his counsel in chapter 4. For now Paul speaks to us about the joy we can have despite the disappointments people can bring.

His counsel in these verses is to think about who you are and what you have been given by the Lord; to stop walking in the flesh and put on the mind of Christ; and to look at life as our Lord Jesus did. The result will be that you will have joy even when people aren't everything they should be—when they fail you, let you down, or hurt you with their words or actions. Jesus was surrounded by people who failed Him, others who had it out for Him, and still others who sought to kill Him and yet, Jesus had fullness of joy. So let's turn to Philippians chapter 2 and read what Paul would have us to learn about the joy of the Lord in the midst of often-difficult people who could certainly steal our joy away.

*Therefore if there is any consolation in Christ, if any comfort of love, if any fellowship of the Spirit, if any affection and mercy, fulfill my joy by being like-minded, having the same love, being of one accord, of one mind. Let nothing be done through selfish ambition or conceit, but in lowliness of mind let each esteem others better than himself. Let each of you look out not only for his own interests, but also for the interests of others.*

*—Philippians 2:1-4*

Paul begins by asking the Philippian believers to consider whether they had experienced any benefits in their relationship with Jesus. The word "consolation" is the Greek word *paraklesis* and speaks of one who "comes alongside to help." Have you ever benefitted by Jesus standing by you when you needed Him? Do you remember all the times you looked around and saw no one but Him?

The word "comfort" in Greek is *paramuthion* and, in this context, speaks of incentive to love others because of the way God has loved you. Is there any incentive found to love others in the fact that He doesn't keep a record of your wrongs, but has put them as far away from Him as the east is from the west? That He continually forgives you when you ask and washes away your sins by the blood of the Lamb? Does that motivate you to keep short lists and offer mercy to others quickly and often? Have you had any benefit by Jesus standing next to you and washing your slate again and again?

Is there any *koinonia*, or "fellowship of His Spirit?" Do you sense the Holy Spirit's intimate participation in your life? Has He assured you of your stand before God and comforted your heart? Are you aware of God's presence within you and the peace that brings? Does the affection and mercy of God change your outlook and interaction with others who might fail you, as you have failed the Lord?

Paul says in verse 2 that he would be filled with joy if they had the same outlook, the same kind of love, and the same kind of accord in their relationships with each other as they had benefited from in their relationship with Jesus. "Be likeminded," he says and the word means to look at something with a shared perspective. "Find the common ground you have as the church and have the same agape love. Be driven by the same affections and realize that because you all belong to God, you are to serve Him together. Think the same way; have the same love; pursue the same goals."

I don't think Paul would have been satisfied with these two women whom he will speak of in Chapter 4 simply mending fences. He sought to eliminate altogether the division that the enemy would use against them. Any differences you and I might have are of far less consequence than the goals God has set before us to reach the world. We are asked to forgive others less than what God has forgiven us (Matthew 18:23-35). We have an obligation to the Lord to now extend the mercy we have received, to others who need it from us. So the Lord, through Paul, challenges us: "Knowing all the benefits you have received since you were saved, now extend those same benefits to each other."

Paul turns in verse 3 to say, "Let nothing be done through selfish ambition (strife)." We saw this word in Philippians 1:15 as Paul spoke of the reasons some were out preaching the Word while Paul was in jail. This word for strife, translated selfish ambition here, is the Greek word for going on the campaign trail. Paul says, "Don't do anything that promotes you. Don't do anything in the church that will push you to the forefront. Don't do anything that will bring you out where all can see you."

The word "conceit" sometimes translated vainglory speaks of empty self-ambition, or self-interest, that dominates the heart but leads us nowhere. There is no satisfaction at the end of this road, no fruit for a life lived this way. Don't do anything as a church, in the church, with the church, by the church, or through the church that would push you to prominence. For self-interest is to have no part in the body of Christ and will only leave you empty and unfulfilled, no matter how you think otherwise. "Check your motives," Paul says.

If everything you do is for you, conflict is inevitable. Instead, Paul's advice is, "Through lowliness of mind, let everyone esteem others better than themselves." I'm thinking this is not the Bible verse you have placed on your refrigerator or car dashboard as your next memory verse. "God loves me." Yes! "God blesses me." Yes! "God's for me." Yes! "Put others first." Not so sure. "Rather than serving yourselves," Paul says, "come with great humility – a deep understanding of who you are and what you are – and put others first. With humility or lowliness of mind, esteem others better than yourself."

Humility is not denying the work God is doing in your life. It is certainly not denying the gifts God has given you to serve Him. To say to someone, when God has given you the gift to sing, "Oh, no, I don't really sing that well," is not humility. It's better to say, "Yes, God has blessed me with a good voice and if I can use it for Him, that would be my joy and goal." Humility doesn't mean I don't recognize any good that I have. It means I recognize any good that I have comes from God so that He might be honored.

When Andrew Murray was asked for his definition of humility, he said, "Humility isn't thinking less of yourself; it's just not thinking of yourself at all." That's a good definition. I don't need to be honored for the gifts God has given me. I need Him to be honored for the gifts He has given me. That's humility. So Paul says, "Don't do things for you. Do them for others and do them for the Lord. Put others before yourself." How this would change the church! Yet, unfortunately, how far from this we often are.

To esteem others better than ourselves literally means to count them higher in the sense of promoting them before yourself, and putting them ahead of you. Esteeming others better than myself isn't some foolish outlook where I approve of those living in sin. Nor does it mean I am at everyone's beck and call whenever they want something. But it certainly means valuing others over myself when it comes to their needs and lives.

God's desire for the church is that we have a genuine regard and love for one another and that we would each choose to put the needs of others before ourselves, regardless of the cost. But has that been your experience in the church? Most people come to church as consumers, asking, "What can it do for me? What can I get out of it? How do I feel when I leave?" But you can't come like that to the Body for any length of time and expect to be satisfied because that's not God's plan for the church. His plan is that you die to yourself and promote another and, through that, His love enables and strengthens you, resulting in your own needs being met.

Humility doesn't mean that I see others as superior. It means that their needs should be greater to me than my own. It means that I have placed them ahead of myself. Humility is the opposite of the selfish ambition and conceit of verse 3. It takes the position of a servant and it fills the heart with joy. The attitude of the servant is to ask, "How can I help? How can I encourage? How can I bless? How can I lift up? How can I move someone forward even if it means leaving myself behind?"

Paul's word to this church comes from a jail cell in Rome where he could soon be executed. He might not have much longer and so his focus is on delivering to them some final words, last words, things of utmost importance — and this is what he gives us. He focuses on the most important and says to us: "You have got to let someone else go first. Unselfish living removes strife."

After God blessed them both with great abundance, Abraham would have to turn and say to Lot in Genesis 13, "We shouldn't be striving. We are family. But your herdsmen are fighting with mine and we have this whole land before us. I think the best thing we should do is separate ourselves. You pick, Lot. If you go left, I'll go right, or vice versa. We just have to find peace because we are one family." The Bible says Lot lifted up his eyes and looked towards the Jordan plains and seeing that they were well watered and beautiful, chose them for himself. He chose the oasis in the desert and offered to Abraham the desert. Yet Abraham had let him take his pick. Lot chose the valley and pitched his tent toward Sodom. But the Lord appeared to Abraham after Lot left and said, "Abraham, look up now with your eyes from the place you are standing. Look north and south, east and west. Walk through the whole land for it is all yours."

How did Abraham realize such an inheritance? Not arguing with Lot. "Hey, I'm older than you. I brought you here and have taken care of you! Who do you think you are, you little selfish kid?" Instead he humbled himself, knowing God was in charge: "Take whatever you want. I just want peace – even if it means loss – because we are family." In response, the Lord proclaimed to him: "It's all yours, Abraham. You haven't lost a thing." Lot looked out for himself and found sin, destruction, and loss. Abraham died to himself for the sake of unity and wouldn't lose a thing, but would gain the world so to speak — first in promise and through later generations, in reality.

Paul says the same thing here in our text: You have to actively put others before yourself. It's such an important issue, Paul now gives four distinct examples of those who had lived, or were living that way, in order to convince the church at Philippi that death to self brought life from God. His first example is Jesus – who came from the glory of heaven to the darkness of earth, who put Himself in a human body to die a horrible death, all for our sakes. His was the ultimate sacrifice. He is the perfect illustration of how to put others before yourself, to do nothing through selfish ambition or conceit, to have the same mind God has towards us. Through Him we will see the result of dying to self is to gain all.

❑ Day Sixteen Complete – Date: _______________________________

Application: ___________________________________

_______________________________________________

_______________________________________________

_______________________________________________

# Philippians 2:5-11
# Day Seventeen

*Let this mind be in you which was also in Christ Jesus, who, being in the form of God, did not consider it robbery to be equal with God, but made Himself of no reputation, taking the form of a bondservant, and coming in the likeness of men. And being found in appearance as a man, He humbled Himself and became obedient to the point of death, even the death of the cross.*

*—Philippians 2:5-8*

"Let this mind be in you." The Greek word for mind is *phroneo* and means to "regard" or have "a certain outlook." Here, Paul gives us, in a few verses, four aspects of the mind or outlook of Christ. The first is that Jesus didn't think of Himself but thought of us when He came from glory to the earth. Had God acted towards us the way we often act towards others, we would all still be dead in our sins. Had God thought like us, He may well have said: "I'd like to come help you but that would mean leaving the comfort of heaven. I'd have to give up the clicker and my recliner. I'd have to come down there and be mistreated. I'd have to die. I'm not going. Sorry, I love you – but not that much."

Thankfully, Jesus is not at all like us. He was in the form of God or, in Greek, *morphe theos*. Though externally He was fashioned like a man, he took a body like ours. In every way, Jesus is still God. And, as God, He doesn't need anything. He has everything. He is part of the Godhead. His praise comes from the angels in heaven. As God, He is dependent upon no one. His position was self-sufficient. His only purpose or reason for coming to the earth would have been for others, not for Himself.

The word "robbery," *harpagmos*, means something to be seized as a prize or to be retained as a reward. Though by nature, Jesus was God! He didn't see that position as something He would have to seize or retain at all costs. Instead, He laid all that down, and left that all behind so he might come and be our Savior, our Redeemer! "He made Himself of no reputation!" So: "Let this mind be in you that was also in Christ Jesus." I certainly can't begin to demand my rights if I stop to think about where Jesus was and what He did to come for me. He is God in heaven and yet came to the earth to suffer and die on my behalf. And all I am being asked to do now, as His child, is to put up with you. And all you have been asked to do, in love, is to put up with me. It seems like small potatoes when I consider what God sacrificed to save me. I now have to deny myself for the benefit of others even as my Lord Jesus denied Himself for all of us. For Him, the cost was enormous!  What does it really cost me, by comparison, to give up my rights for you? So what if I don't get my way once in a while? So what if people don't like my ideas? The calling and goals set before the church by the Lord are so important that nothing should get in the way of their accomplishment. The people of the world are dying and headed for judgment in their sins and our lives revolve around ourselves rather than considering the lost for which Jesus came. Had God treated us that way, we'd still be here crying out for help with no help available.

"Let this mind be in you that was also in Christ Jesus." Though Jesus was equal with God, He didn't retain His position for Himself but made Himself of no reputation. By comparison we read about the fall of the devil from glory. In Isaiah 14, we read of Satan's fall and the Lord said to him, "You said in your heart that you would ascend into heaven, that you would be like the Most High, that you would exalt your throne above the stars of God, that you would sit in the mountain of the congregation, that you would ascend to the heights of the clouds." Yet it was those five "I wills" that brought him down to hell. He saw the position of God as something to be grasped like a plunderer's prize and it brought a great eternal fall.

Satan grasped at the position of God. Jesus made Himself of no reputation, instead taking upon Himself the form of a servant. You see, it is not simply enough to think about others if you don't act upon that understanding. Jesus, being God, didn't see the need to grasp or hold onto His position. He thought of others and then He came to serve them. The Greek words literally read: He emptied Himself. What did He empty Himself of? His deity? No. If you have Jesus emptying Himself of His deity, you no longer have a Savior that is God. He is fully God. So, what did He empty Himself of? He emptied Himself of His glory and the independent use of His divine attributes. In other words, Jesus didn't perform any miracles upon the earth as Jesus, the Son of God. He came as Jesus, the Son of Man, moved by the Holy Spirit, so He could be our example. He purposefully limited Himself so that He might be in every way tempted like we are; so that we could have a great High Priest that was touched with the feelings of our infirmities; so He could relate to our struggles.

Jesus would say to His disciples, "It's a good thing for you that I'm leaving so I can send the Holy Spirit. This 'living in the body' thing won't work. I'll be limited. I'll be over here and can't be over there. So the Spirit of God will come and fill you all."

Jesus limited Himself for 33 years. He emptied Himself of His position–His honor, His power, His glory, and His freedom. He took upon Himself the form of a servant. He went from *morphe theos*, form of God, to *morphe doulous*, form of a bondslave. Why? So He could redeem us.

The phrase "found in appearance as a man" in verse 8 is the Greek word, *schema*, which speaks of external appearance. How did people see Jesus? He looked like them. He was a baby. He grew up. He went to school. He had a family, friends, and a trade. He shed tears. He was destined to die.

As Christians, we can't wait to go to heaven, where there will be no more tears, no more harshness, no more bitterness, no more devil. It's going to be great. Isn't that what we are looking forward to? Isn't that what keeps you going every day? Yet Jesus left that very place to come here, because if He didn't come, you would never be able to go there. But He came to serve and save each of you. Let this mind be in you.

What grace! That Jesus would humble Himself and obey the will of His Father even to the point of death on a cross. He came to die painfully and shamefully. He came to be our sin offering, a Lamb without spot, to redeem us. Let this mind be in you. What was His purpose for coming? Was it for His benefit? No, it was for ours. We had not accomplished one thing to convince God we were worth saving except to curse Him and grumble about Him, to speak evil of Him, and to live our own way. What grace! From heaven He came to earth. From glory He came to shame. From master to servant, from life to death. He didn't have to do it. He didn't have to die. He did so because He wanted to save. Remember that the next time you're about to say, "I have forgiven you for the last time," or, "I'm not going to take it anymore." Lay those words next to these: Jesus came from heaven to earth! Let this mind be in you!

In the church, we often find pride, selfishness, and a real unwillingness to have the mind of Christ. It is the single thing the enemy often uses to divide. Jesus came thinking of us, came to serve us, and came to sacrifice Himself on our behalf. We are often willing to serve only while it is convenient to us. I find that true even in the Body of Christ. Yet Jesus suffered the loss of all things to save us. He lost absolutely everything and set every bit of it aside so that you and I would have a future and a hope. Let this mind be in you!

There was a religious festival several years ago in Brazil, where religious artifacts were being sold. One of the signs read "Cheap Crosses" and the reporter commenting on it in his article said he felt that was what many Christians were looking for: a cheap cross. "Can I be saved and walk with God without it costing me anything?" they ask. "I'd like that – not too much cost." Jesus' cross was hardly cheap. It cost Him everything. Your cross to bear will not be cheap, either, if you are going to take your place among the Body and be the peacemaker God is going to use. But it will never rise to the cost paid for you!

Paul says, be like-minded. Have the same love. Be of one accord. Live your life for the sake of another's benefit. Look at Jesus. Look what He did.

*Therefore God also has highly exalted Him and given Him the name which is above every name, that at the name of Jesus every knee should bow, of those in heaven, and of those on earth, and of those under the earth, and that every tongue should confess that Jesus Christ is Lord, to the glory of God the Father.*
*—Philippians 2:9-11*

What happened when Jesus gave it all up, let it all go, and died to all He had? He found great glory from His Father. He was exalted above every name. Like Abraham who was offered all the land for dying to himself, Jesus is given a name above every name. Every knee will bow; every tongue confess in heaven, hell, and on the earth. Oh, they're not saying it yet but they will. Everyone will one day confess that Jesus is the Lord.

Why do we have divisions in the church? A primary cause is our unwillingness to have the mind of Christ. We want the benefits of His sacrifice without the cost of now following His example by serving rather than being served. Yet Jesus' example would say that the way you honor the Lord will be the way the Lord exalts you. What do men say about Jesus? They ridicule Him. They slander Him. They speak evil of Him. They accuse Him – and then the Father gives Him a name above every other name. One day, according to Isaiah, all of the world will bow their knee to confess who He is.

"Humble yourselves in the sight of the Lord, and He will lift you up," James 4:10. When are you lifted up? As you lay down your life for the sake of others. The way up with God is always down. For 13 years, Joseph suffered through one unjust circumstance to another. Yet even in the worst of times, he remained faithful to the Lord and in serving others, overcoming evil with good. The result would eventually be seen. Eventually! He would rise, through God's hand being upon him, to be second in command to Pharaoh and the deliverer of the Jewish people. David was anointed king 14-and-a-half years before he ever saw the throne completely in his power. But he served the Lord faithfully as he waited, often on the run and in fear for his own life. The result? God used him as the greatest king in Israel's history.

Paul's concern for the church was that if the enemy got a foothold in the area of self and selfishness, it would be extremely difficult to be fruitful or joyful in the body. The way to joy, even when people aren't always fair, is to have the mind of Christ and serve those who don't love you, bless those who hate you, and lay your life down for those who don't want anything to do with you. Do it again and again because Jesus did that for you and now calls you to serve Him in this way. As a result, joy will be your strength. Counseling in the church as we know it would stop, for 95 percent of counseling is really people trying to get you to take their side in areas of conflict.

Be like-minded, Paul says. Do it with humility. Put others ahead of yourself. Look to see what they need and not what you need. Be like Jesus. If you find yourself in conflict with people, you might take this to heart because it seems to me that you don't need two to make peace. You only need one. You need two to fight, but only one to make peace. God came, though we were at war with Him, to make peace. We need to have the mind of Christ, one that thinks of others first.

❏ Day Seventeen Complete – Date: _______________________________

Application: _______________________________________________

123

_______________________________________________

_______________________________________________

_______________________________________________

# Philippians 2:12-13
# Day Eighteen

*Therefore, my beloved, as you have always obeyed, not as in my presence only, but now much more in my absence, work out your own salvation with fear and trembling; for it is God who works in you both to will and to do for His good pleasure.*

*—Philippians 2:12-13*

In verse 12, Paul compliments the Philippian believers on their diligence in seeking the Lord over the years. It would appear that there might have been a tendency in the Philippian church to lean too heavily upon Paul – on his advice, his counsel, his ideas. We still see that in the church. You look to someone who helps you and, pretty soon, you can't make up your mind without them. But if he were put to death, the Philippian church wouldn't have Paul to lean on anymore. He says clearly to them, "You have always done well when I was around, now you are going to have to work this thing out on your own."

This phrase "work out," *katergazomai* in Greek, means, "with continued, sustained, strenuous, ongoing effort." Now, before you conclude Paul was telling them to work for their salvation, verse 13 quickly adds that it is God who works in us to will and to do of His good pleasure. Within the context of the verse here, the Philippians were already saved and had shown the fruit of their salvation through obedience. They had been walking with the Lord. The Holy Spirit already dwelt in them and had fallen upon them. And that is Paul's point: Because you are saved, because God dwells in you and is with you and has fallen upon you, you don't need my help for everything. You are going to have to learn to stand on your own two feet. And you will have to put in the effort to live out the salvation that you have in Christ – in your lifestyle, in the decisions you make, and in the activities you pursue. God will help you, but you are going to have to put into practice having the mind of Christ.

Paul's injunction to this fairly young church is not that they work for their salvation. It's not that they work towards their salvation. It's that they work out that which God was already working in them. "Learn to hear from the Lord yourself," he said. "Learn to listen for what God might want to say to you. Learn to find out together what it is that God wants."

There is a big Biblical word for that, "sanctification." It's means to be "set apart," "to be made holy," or "to be reserved for exclusive use." Once you are saved, God justifies you immediately. You are "justified" – just as if you'd never sinned. God clears the slate. Your sins are forgiven; your eternal future is secure. God has made you whole and new through your faith in His Son. But sanctification has only begun.

The moment you come to the Lord, many things change in a moment's time. You pass from death to life. You were blind but now you see. The minute I cried, "Save me Lord Jesus," I passed from the kingdom of darkness into the kingdom of God's dear Son immediately. However, in many ways, I am still very much the same. I still have to deal with the habits I have had all my life. The work of God's Spirit in my life in teaching me His ways now needs to be applied to the way I make decisions. Whereas before, I would run off and do something without thinking, now I have to pray. My doubts are still going to need answers. My hesitation is still going to have to be undergirded with God's strength. The problems that I have will still need solving. Wrong behavior patterns will need to be made right.

So, though I am justified immediately by the blood of

the Lamb and though I have a place to go if I were to drop dead, God wants to begin to bring me to a place where the things I have from Him and know about Him impact who I am. In other words, He takes over my life and, little by little, it begins to show. What Paul is saying to this church is, "You've always done well with me around, but I might not be around all of the time. You can hear from the Lord directly. You can put in the effort to submit your life, your ways, and your practices into His hands."

Sanctification is a life-long process. It is described in the Bible in a couple of ways that tell you this. We are told to run the race with patience. We are told to put on the new man. We are told to fight the good fight of faith. All of those statements say the same thing: once you come to know the Lord, there is the work to be done of taking what God says and acting upon it with His help and His strength. That is why Paul says to the Philippian church, "You guys need to work this thing out. You need to see who you are, what you have been delivered from, and what is driving this selfish behavior. You need to work out your own salvation with an attitude before the Lord of fear and trembling. Let this mind be in you that was also in Christ Jesus."

When we come and give our lives to the Lord Jesus, the Holy Spirit moves in and begins the work of establishing that life of Christ in us. We go to church and God begins to teach us His Word. We get on our knees to pray and God begins to open our understanding. When we disobey, the Lord is there to correct and guide us. In that process I have a decision to make: Am I going to do what God says or not? I have to let God work in my life to the point where my life is His and it shows. And as I surrender to Him, He changes my life each day from glory to glory and from strength to strength.

Yet verse 13 tells me I can't even take any credit for the will to want to surrender to Him, for it is also the Lord who gives me the will and the ability to do as He says. It is He who works in me to do and to will to do. I just have to follow along.

I just have to cooperate with God. God begins to work on my willingness. He gives me spiritual desires and the ability to accomplish them. He focuses my attention on His good pleasure, on what delights or satisfies Him. He brings me to the place where I long to please Him. What a change! I never wanted to please God before. I always wanted to please only me and I hoped that God would be happy in the process. But now I am saved and God begins to work in me to will and to do of His good pleasure.

One of the greatest blessings of surrendering my life to the Lord is that I now look forward to His plans for me. I know He wants to do great things through me for His glory. The word *katergazomai*, or "work out", in secular Greek is used to describe those digging in a cave for gold or farmers working a field to gather their crops. It's a word that describes effort with the result of fruit or gain at the end. So, from a secular standpoint, Paul uses a word his readers would easily understand. Dig deep; work long; plant the field. There's lots of potential but you need to work it out yourselves before the Lord with His help. You need to cooperate with the Lord as you take the mind of Christ, live by His strength, and do what He says.

I should tell you that for most Christians, here's where growth stops. We like what God does for us but when we have to start to cooperate, we start to balk. We begin to wonder why things don't move a little faster. Yet know that there are no Biblical shortcuts to becoming a mature Christian – at least none that I have found. There is no way to cheat. There are no "Cliff Notes." You can't get the abridged version. You need to work it out through diligent daily mining or farming with the resources God provides.

It is one thing for a Christian to say, "I do it all for the glory of God," but it is an entirely different thing to actually do it! It is one thing for a Christian to say, "Forgive us our debts as we forgive those who trespass against us," but it's another thing to do it. It's one thing to say, "Jesus is the head of our home," but it's another thing to pray with your family and seek

God's will. You have to work out your own salvation. Oh, in your head it comes quickly but it is in your life that God wants it to show. And it requires your submission to God – not to Paul, not to your pastor, not to your buddy. You and the Lord have to work this thing out. And the way that occurs is with fear and trembling.

Work it out with a reverence for God that will leave you shaking when you realize whom you serve. That is literally the way this is written. It's the kind of reverence that leaves you quivering not because you're afraid, but because you are moved by whom you are standing before. I have to work this out because God is God and He is the One I am serving. He is the One to whom I answer. He is the One that works in me. And now I have to work this thing out humbly and obediently – not complacently, not shabbily, not half-heartedly, but diligently.

Paul writes to the Corinthians in the second chapter of his first letter that he was with them in weakness and in fear, with much trembling. Why would he be afraid of the Corinthians? He wasn't. But he realized the awesome task that he faced. Corinth was a city lost in idolatry and he had to stand up and talk about the Lord. This was a huge challenge for Paul as he had lately faced great physical and emotional suffering for standing up for Jesus in the cities that led him here. It humbled him. When Titus returned from the Corinthians to Paul, he said in his second letter, "And his affections are greater for you as he remembers the obedience of you all, how with fear and trembling you received [Titus]" (2 Corinthians 7:15). In other words, "When you realized that the Lord had sent him to you and it was God's work, you were submissive to the work of God." To Christian slaves he wrote, "Bondservants, be obedient to those who are your masters according to the flesh, with fear and trembling, in sincerity of heart, as to Christ" (Ephesians 6:5). Have the same kind of respect for your masters as you do for the Lord.

Work out the salvation that God is working within. It

has got to come out of your life. And with that attitude, I can find myself doing God's pleasure. In Psalm 40:8, David wrote, "I delight to do your will, O my God." It might not have started that way. I delighted in anything but doing the will of God, but obediently I have now come to the point that His will is indeed my delight. I wish I could convince every believer that church attendance and involvement along with Bible study and daily prayer will keep them close to Jesus because they are working out their own salvation obediently with fear and trembling by doing these things. I am not always successful at convincing them of this – but I know it is true for each of us.

You need to be in the Word. You need to be in fellowship. I guarantee that if you look at everyone who walks with the Lord in a half-hearted manner, you will see the difference. This process of working out our salvation with fear and trembling is to take place in the world so that, as we change, the world notices. They see what God is doing and will seek to believe and know Him as well.

❑ Day Eighteen Complete – Date: _______________________________

Application: _________________________________________________

_________________________________________________________

_________________________________________________________

_________________________________________________________

# Philippians 2:14-18
## Day Nineteen

*Do all things without complaining and disputing, that you may become blameless and harmless, children of God without fault in the midst of a crooked and perverse generation, among whom you shine as lights in the world, holding fast the word of life, so that I may rejoice in the day of Christ that I have not run in vain or labored in vain.*

*—Philippians 2:14-16*

We are to do all things without complaining or disputing. You can obey willfully or you can obey defiantly. As we were getting ready to go to church tonight, I said to my dog, "Go outside." He immediately looked at my wife as if to say, "Did he really mean that?" He went out but I am sure that in his mind he was staying in. I wonder sometimes if we don't come to church like that. We're here but, in our minds, we're at home. It's like the little kid told to sit in the corner. "I'll go to the corner," he thinks, "but in my mind I will still be standing up."

As you set out to walk with God in obedience, do things without murmuring, muttering, or arguing. That's His advice to you and me as Christians in the world. Do the work of God, the dictates of God willfully, without any rebellious undertones, without any, "I'll do it but in my mind I'll be standing up."

The word "disputing" is the Greek word for "dialogue" and speaks of inward reasoning. Although it's popular to say, "We've got to get together and talk," that doesn't work well for your walk with God. No talk is necessary! Do it without dialogue, Paul says. God doesn't want to talk about it. He wants you to do it. He would have you listen, not question. He doesn't want you to argue in your heart. He doesn't want inward rebellion. He wants you to do what He says. Isn't that what you want from your children? Well, God even sees rebellion in our hearts and seeks to have us resistance free!

"Do all things without complaining or disputing." The word "complaining" is the Greek word *goggusmos*. Often translated murmuring it describes what happens when inward reasoning surfaces and expresses itself audibly. It's one of those "under your breath" kind of deals. Not only does God not want to talk to you about it – He doesn't want to hear about it from you either. In Luke 5, we're told that the scribes and Pharisees murmured among themselves, saying, "Why does Jesus eat and drink with publicans and sinners?" In Matthew 20, Jesus tells a story about a householder who hired people one morning to work in his field. When some laborers showed up two hours before closing and were paid the same amount as the ones who had worked all day, the early birds started murmuring. God hates murmuring or complaining. It is such a grief to the Lord for it reveals the disposition of the heart, the tendency within to always oppose Him.

Maybe the best example of murmuring is found if you follow Israel out of Egypt. They could have qualified as professional murmurers. They had degrees in murmuring. They could murmur about anything. They came out of Egypt and murmured before they ever passed the Red Sea. Out less than a week, they got thirsty, and what did they do? Pray? No! They murmured. They traveled a bit further and arriving at the wilderness of Sin, they were hungry and so they murmured. Two weeks later at Rephidim, thirst set in and, you guessed it, they murmured all the louder. When they didn't like the manna, they murmured. When the spies came back with bad news, they murmured. Finally, God sent snakes into the camp to bite them in order to stop their murmuring.

But how much different are they from us? God blesses us and we complain about something else. He blesses us again and we still are not satisfied. God lays out His direction and we do it – but we go kicking and screaming. Paul says, "If you are going to work out your own salvation in the eyes of a world that's watching you, you had better quit murmuring." Instead of murmuring and disputing, we are to obey with fear and trembling. If we do that, the world will see the Lord, we will have peace, and God will work out His salvation in us.

We are to live as children of God without rebuke, or fault – a phrase which speaks of our relationship with Him. In other words, not only are you living without complaining or disputing, but also as the children of God, you are maintaining open lines of communication and fellowship between you and the Lord and there is no barrier between you. To say the least, living like this in His light will bear significant fruit in a world that is lost and dark. In fact, the words Paul uses to describe the world is that it is bent and warped by sin – a perverse generation, a world of people turned askew from the things of God. You used to be like that. You were bent and turned by sin until God's Word and God's Spirit straightened you out. Now, those still bent over in sin watch you work out your own salvation with fear and trembling. When you face a trial and people at work hear you say, "God has saved me; I belong to Him; He's not going to let me down," their crookedness becomes attracted to you as you live out the life of God before their eyes – blameless and harmless and straightened in heart by His work in you.

Blameless means there is nothing that can be judged by others or found to be contrary. Harmless speaks of being genuine, simple, or uncomplicated. Your life is an open book. There is no agenda, no formula, no changing. You're just living for the Lord. The crooked watch and the perverse look. The problem for Paul was that if saints were seen bickering, complaining, and gossiping, or selfish, argumentative, rude, and slow to obey God, it would leave a horrible witness in the eyes of the community. So he says, "Knock it off. Have this mind of Christ. Deny yourself. Esteem others better than yourself. Look on the things of others, not just on your own things. Work out your salvation with fear and trembling and be those blameless and harmless saints shining as lights in a perverse, bent, crooked world." That's why Paul says you should work out your own salvation with fear and trembling as God works in you to do and to will to do of His good pleasure, that you should be harmless and blameless—so that the world has no reason to criticize you except for your faith in God, which actively works itself out in your life. They can say you are a fool for believing; they can say you are weak; they can say you need a crutch. But that is all they should be able to say about you because your life is so attractive as they behold the joy, peace, hope, and confidence God has given to you!

Paul literally cries here, "Quit fighting, for crying out loud, there is a far bigger issue here than your little beef." In fact, in verse 15, he told the Philippian believers they were to shine as lights in the world. In Daniel 6, we read that, although the princes of Babylon hated Daniel, they couldn't find any fault in him because he was faithful. They came to the conclusion that the only way they could bring charges against him was through the way he obeyed the law of God. To this end, they told the king to sign a law prohibiting his subjects to pray to anyone but him for 30 days as proof that he was the supreme ruler. The king signed the law and it wasn't long before he was told that Daniel was still praying to God. The king's heart was broken because he liked Daniel. He had been hustled. As one who was blameless and harmless, the one and only way Daniel would ever offend was by staying consistent to his faith in God. If only the church could live like that.

Christians can be and often are, targeted for their faith, but what if the criticism is deserved? We deserve to be called money-grubbers if that's the kind of faith we show the world. If we lie through our teeth, the world has the right to criticize us. And that is what Paul is saying. The church shouldn't be on the chopping block because we play the hypocrite. The church should be a shining light in a perverse world. The church should be filled with harmless and blameless people who don't murmur, who don't dispute, and who daily work out the salvation that God is working in them. The world is watching.

Paul goes on to say we are to hold fast the word of life. The word holding, *epecho*, means "to apply" or to "put practices into action." It is a call to put theory to work. It's where the rubber meets the road. It's one thing to preach to people but that doesn't sell anybody on anything. That's why, when you go to the fair and see the latest kitchen utensil, they can't just tell you about it, it has to be seen slicing and dicing. It's when you see it that you want it. Holding fast the word of life says, "Look what happens when you walk with God. Look at the joy of the Lord. Look at the peace in the midst of darkness. Look at the self-control and the selflessness. Look at the love and the joy." Let the world watch.

Paul continues, "If you do that, then one day when I stand before the Lord, I will rejoice that I haven't run or labored in vain amongst you. The world will see you working out with fear and trembling and the crooked will want to be made straight." The word Paul uses for "run" is the word for marathon and the word he uses for "labor" is a word that speaks of laboring to the point of exhaustion. "All of my efforts will not have been in vain if, in that day, gathered together before the Lord, you have plenty of fruit to present to Him," Paul says.

> *Yes, and if I am being poured out as a drink offering on the sacrifice and service of your faith, I am glad and rejoice with you all. For the same reason you also be glad and rejoice with me.*
>
> *—Philippians 2:17-18*

The word "poured out" is *spendo* and is the normal word used in the Old Testament for the drink offering of wine that God commanded was to accompany various sacrifices

(Numbers 15). Whenever the wine was placed with burnt offerings and peace offerings, it was to denote that the sacrifice was one made with joy. Here, Paul uses that word to refer to himself. "If I am to be the drink offering that is poured out, as long as you are the main offering, I will be the joyful one watching you do these things in the Lord. I'll be the accompaniment. And if that means I die while you offer yourself to God, I'll gladly be the poured-out drink offering. That will be joyful to me and it ought to bring joy to you. We have a stake in each other. I'm bringing the Gospel. You're supporting the work that I have done for years. We're in this thing together." Amen! What an example! Be like Jesus; let this mind be in you!

❏ Day Nineteen Complete – Date: _______________________________

Application: _______________________________________________

_______________________________________________

_______________________________________________

_______________________________________________

# Philippians 2:19-21
## Day Twenty

*But I trust in the Lord Jesus to send Timothy to you shortly, that I also may be encouraged when I know your state. For I have no one like-minded, who will sincerely care for your state.*
*—Philippians 2:19-20*

Paul now turns to give us a third example of these truths as seen in the life of Timothy. Having pointed to Jesus and spoken of his own life in ministry, Paul now holds up his younger protégé before us to teach the same lesson again: let this mind be in you that was also in Christ Jesus. Epaphroditus had come from Philippi to Paul and told him of the church's concern for him. "How you are doing, how you are feeling, how you are holding up? Is everything all right with you? Can you handle it?" And Paul writes back, "I hope to send Timothy to you shortly so I can find out how you are doing."

From what we read of Timothy here and in other places, it seems to me that he was probably the least likely fellow that Paul could afford to send them. Under house arrest in Rome, unable to get out or get around, Paul had Timothy at his beck and call. He was his right arm. Losing Timothy would leave Paul high and dry because, according to 2 Timothy 4, when he was arrested the first time, everyone forsook him except Timothy. Yet Paul writes, "I want to send Timothy to you. I hope shortly to send him your way." What a sacrifice that would have been for Paul to send them someone of Timothy's caliber! He was a guy Paul could ill afford to lose, just to find out how they were doing. That was God's love working through the apostle Paul in jail in Rome.

The Scriptures tell us Timothy was a man whose mother and grandmother had both come to know the Lord through God's Word. As a result, Timothy had been taught the Scriptures from a very young age. We read in Acts 16 that Timothy's mother was a believer but that his dad, being Greek, was a pantheist. We are not told how the ladies in the house had come to know the Lord but only that they had and had passed along to Timothy their faith in Christ. Paul first met young Timothy on his first trip through Iconium. It appears that Timothy came to a service and, listening to Paul preach, got saved. It was in Iconium during those meetings that Paul was dragged out of town, stoned, and left for dead by some Jewish sympathizers who hated what he was teaching. It could be that Timothy saw the whole thing, though history tells us that these towns were so big that something could happen in one corner without the other corner hearing about it.

Paul continued on in his travels and went back to his home church and it was about six years later that Paul would head this way again on his second missionary journey. When he arrived this time, he began to ask around about what God was doing in the church and everyone brought up Timothy, a young man after God's own heart who had a good reputation, a servant's heart and was being used mightily by the Lord. So Paul goes to find Timothy because he needed someone to take the place of John Mark, who had failed him on his first trip. Paul asked Timothy if he would be willing to go with him, while warning him how difficult the path would be. When Timothy agreed, Paul had him circumcised so the Jews would be more prone to listen to him. Timothy comes on board and his job early on was to carry bags, make reservations, and run errands for Paul and Silas.

As you look at Timothy's participation in the work of God, you discover that this mind of Christ that God wants each of us to have doesn't develop overnight. It is the work of God that He accomplishes in you as you faithfully walk with

Him each day. Timothy's development as a Christian wasn't automatic, but over time, God began to cultivate in this young man's heart a great work of His Spirit, and he began to grow. Paul would take great pride in Timothy. More than once, he would refer to Timothy as his son in the faith because Paul had been the one who had led him to the Lord. If you follow Timothy through the Book of Acts, you see him go to Philippi, Thessalonica, and Berea. Then Paul says, "You stay here with Silas for awhile. I'll go ahead to Athens and you can catch up with me there." Timothy had no sooner arrived in Athens than Paul said, "You have to go back to Thessalonica and see how they are doing. Then meet me in Corinth." Timothy was running all over the place serving the Lord, faithful in the little!

According to Eusebius, a well-respected early church historian, Timothy became the first bishop, or pastor, of the church of Ephesus. While serving there, we are told that he was clubbed to death by a crowd for speaking out against the evils of idolatry during one of the feasts to Diana. Timothy had become well persuaded that serving the Lord was the way to go. But it didn't happen overnight. Reading about him in a few chapters of Acts only takes us a matter of minutes. You don't realize that you have just covered 15 years of his life. But here he is, faithfully staying with Paul when everyone else deserted him.

Timothy paid his dues and over time grew into the place of effective servant. In these next few verses, Paul gives us three qualities of Timothy relating to our topic: joy and service to God's people.

> *For I have no one like-minded, who will sincerely care for your state. For all seek their own, not the things which are of Christ Jesus.*
> *—Philippians 2:20-21*

I have to believe that there are few people in any age who are as committed to the Lord as Paul, as displayed in the way he behaved himself and lived his life along with his genuine sacrifice and deep concern for the spiritual welfare of others. Or his willingness to return to a town and a people that had beat him up and left him for dead. Paul lived his life willing to lay it down for the flock of Jesus. I would suspect that you would find few pastors willing to do that. And Paul pays Timothy the ultimate compliment when he writes, "Here is one man I would trust with everything. I would send him to represent me, and the Lord as well, without hesitancy. I have no other man as like-minded as he." In the church at that time in Rome, there were thousands of Christians. But in Paul's honest opinion, none of them measured up to Timothy. Maybe some of them had the time, but they didn't have the temperament. Others may have had the heart, but they didn't have the opportunity. But more than that, Paul saw that most everyone sought their own way rather than the things of the Lord.

If there is a glaring weakness in the visible church, it has always been the lack of commitment and dedication on the part of the people of God for the things of God. Don't think however that this is a recent problem. Here Paul is in jail, on death row, and writes, "The problem is I only have one guy I can send out of a whole church."

"The harvest is great but the laborers are few," Jesus said. "Pray to the Lord of the harvest that He send forth laborers." In fact, the Gospels record that Jesus used this exact same verse three different times in his earthly ministry. In Luke 10, He spoke to His disciples about the harvest being ready. In John 4, the disciples said to Jesus in no uncertain terms that any ministry in Samaria would require a lot of advance work because the Samaritans never got anything right. Yet Jesus said to them, "No, the harvest is white. It's the laborers who are lacking." In Matthew 9 it was as Jesus was walking through Galilee that, when He looked at the people as sheep without a shepherd, was He moved with compassion and said to the disciples, "The harvest is ripe. What we need to do is pray for laborers."

In three different places at three different times from three different experiences, Jesus said the same thing. And when God repeats Himself, it is because it's a lesson we want to learn well, and reputation is a good teacher. When He tells us three times to pray for laborers, we better start praying for laborers! Jesus' view of the willingness of the lost to hear and their willingness to be reached was far different from anyone that walked with Him. He saw people as being ready. We see people as either hard or impossible to reach. But Jesus says, "Don't assume it will take months to get to harvest or that it will require work and time and waiting and struggle and strife." The problem isn't the readiness of the harvest – it's the readiness of the laborers. If the harvest is great and it is the laborers that are few, then we can only conclude that we're not doing anything, rather than that there is nothing for us to do or no place for us to serve. Jesus said there is plenty to do. He just doesn't have enough people to do it.

Timothy was a young man who had the mind of Christ, who wasn't just a hearer of the Word but a doer, and he had learned what a servant was through years of keeping up with Paul's schedule. Whether the church is 50 people or 5,000, the majority of the work is always done by only a small percentage. In the area of finances, it is the few who give and support the many. In the area of outreach, it is the few who go out while the many rejoice at their fruit. In the area of labor, it's the few who are available and the many who are too busy for the task. There are plenty of attendees in the church but the sitters far outnumber the doers. It's always that way. Paul says, "I would love to send you more guys than Timothy, but he's the only one I know who is more interested in the lost than in himself, more interested in serving than being served" (Mark 10:45).

In Luke 9, Jesus addresses this issue of the willingness of people to only be hearers of the Word. We read about a man who told Jesus he'd follow Him wherever He went. That's a great promise, but Jesus challenged him by telling him that, although foxes have holes and birds have nests, the Son of Man had nowhere to lay His head. In other words, following Jesus wasn't easy. It wouldn't be mansions. It would be rocks for pillows. We all have good intentions but getting things moving is hard. We mean well but God doesn't base His rewards on intentions.

In verse 59 of Luke 9 we read, "Then He said to another, 'Follow Me.' But he said, 'Lord, let me first go and bury my father.'" The first man had volunteered and Jesus told him to count the cost. Here, this one was invited by Jesus, "Come and follow Me," only to have this second man make an argument for procrastination. From the way it is written, it would seem that his father wasn't dead yet – maybe not even close. In other words, the man was saying, " I have other things to do but there will come a time one day, someday, sometime, somewhere when You least expect it and I'll show up to serve. I'd like to follow You, Lord but right now there are other matters in my life that are more pressing. I don't want to come now, but I would like to keep my options open. Could I get a reservation for sometime down the road? Maybe when my kids are grown, when my job situation is better, when my time is less valuable?"

There are many like that who follow in word only – and then there are the Timothys. No wonder Paul lamented, "I don't have anyone like him." He is a rare breed. Most people are too selfish or too concerned about themselves and not nearly concerned enough about the lost for whom Jesus died!

Jesus' answer to the man in Luke 9 was to let the dead bury the dead, to value the spiritual over the temporal, and to quit making excuses. In Luke 9:61, we read, "And another also said, 'Lord, I will follow You, but let me first go and bid them farewell who are at my house.'"

"Let me first." The man who wanted to bury his father first had said a similar thing and now this third man cries, "Let me first say goodbye to my family." If your life of serving God is "let me first ..." you are going to miss the boat. "Let me first" won't work. Paul knew many that would serve in that manner. But he only knew one, Timothy, willing to be a servant. If you want to have joy, you have to become a servant. There's certainly nothing wrong with telling your family goodbye except that obviously wasn't the issue. The issue was, "Lord, I have other things to do. I have loyalties at home and loyalties to the world in addition to my loyalty to You."

In response to what He saw in this man's heart, Jesus tells him that no man, having put his hand to the plow and looking back, is fit for the kingdom of God. It is one thing to look back to see if the plow is furrowing a straight line. But you can't plow looking back. Jesus' lesson for us from these three with such half-hearted intentions was: You have to be single-minded. You need to be a servant who says, "Lord, whatever You want." What a big difference between, "Lord, whatever You want" and "Let me first ..." And you could see that difference without squinting! You see the talkers and the doers – the guys who will spin a web and those that will actually get down and do the work. You know the difference – so did Paul. And he knew Timothy fell into the right category.

Chapter 1, verse 21 says, "For to me, to live is Christ, and to die is gain." Chapter 2, verse 21 says, "For all seek their own, not the things which are of Christ Jesus." Are you a "1:21" or a "2:21" person?

"For this reason I have sent Timothy to you," Paul wrote to the Corinthians. "He is my beloved son and faithful in the Lord and he will teach you the ways of Christ as I have been teaching in every church." What a good thing to hear if you are Timothy – especially when, from all that we know from Scripture, Timothy was still a young man who could be easily intimidated. He was quiet, withdrawn, reserved, a timid individual who probably wouldn't raise his voice in a room full of noise. Read 1 Timothy 4 and 2 Timothy 1 and you will hear Paul's counsel to him about this. "Come on, Timothy, stand up. Be an example. Stir up the gift within you. Don't let these guys intimidate you just because you are younger. God is going to use you. Stick with it."

Paul was a different breed – yet says of Timothy, "He's my beloved son. He's just like me." How? Timothy's personality wasn't like Paul's but his heart was. They were both servants. "He will sincerely care for your state," verse 20 tells us. In the KJV it is written, "He will naturally care for your state." Timothy was a natural. It had become second nature for him to put others before himself and not do anything for self-glory. Others had part-time commitments, served God when their schedules allowed, and gave God some of their time. Not Timothy. He was sold out. He didn't have to put on his "I'm a servant" hat. He just was one. He didn't have to be one thing at church and something else at home. It was just his nature to serve. What a wonderful thing to have said about you – that you are a natural servant!

It has been said that the test of a true servant is not how well they handle their responsibilities but what they do with their privileges. People who serve themselves will use their privileges for their own benefit. "I don't have to punch a clock, so I can stay out 10 minutes longer for coffee" or, "I don't need to sit with the regular folks because I am a special individual." The servant will use his privileges to benefit someone else. "Since I don't have to be on the clock, I can come in early to find out if anyone needs help."

Paul said of Timothy that he was a natural. "I don't have to watch him every minute for I know whether I watch or not he will be serving the Lord and His people."

❑ Day Twenty Complete – Date: _______________________________

Application: _______________________________________________

145

_______________________________________________

_______________________________________________

_______________________________________________

# Philippians 2:22-25
# Day Twenty-One

*But you know his proven character, that as a son with his father he served with me in the gospel.*
*—Philippians 2:22*

Although the Philippian church had seen Timothy's faithfulness first-hand, Paul hadn't immediately added Timothy to his ministry team. Once Timothy was saved, Paul's instructions to him were to go to church. And he left him for five or six years. Timothy had to go to church, just like we do. He had to get involved, just like we do. And as he did, the Lord built him up day by day in the pretty mundane things of life. He proved himself at home – through fellowship with the body, through learning the Word, and through obeying God in the days and weeks and months and years that followed. Eventually the church recognized God's hand upon him and when Paul returned, it was Timothy they wanted him to meet. If someone in your church needed some help tonight, would your name come up as someone who could be called? Timothy proved himself with Paul and his team as well — he carried the bags, made reservations, and ran errands. Every day, he learned. Every day, God molded him for what lay ahead.

Years later, when Timothy was pastoring the church in Ephesus, Paul would write him a letter telling him not to appoint a novice as an elder because if the branches go out farther than the roots go down, the tree will fall over. You can't hurry people along. You have to let them grow and watch God work. Over time, you'll be able to differentiate between those who are serving and those who are just talking. If you're an elder, it should be because people recognize that you are doing the work of an elder, not simply because someone has given you a title. You're a deacon because you are actually "deaconing,"–not a real word but certainly a real principle.

Paul followed Jesus' method of training. He balanced teaching with practical application. He gave Timothy on-the-job training. Timothy learned to have the mind of Christ by daily walking with God and serving Paul. Faithful in the little things, he eventually became the pastor of one of the largest churches in the area. As a boy, Timothy had listened to his mom and grandma teach him Bible verses. Years later, he's standing in the pulpit of this huge Ephesian church and sharing with many the good word of God.

*Therefore I hope to send him at once, as soon as I see how it goes with me. But I trust in the Lord that I myself shall also come shortly.*
*—Philippians 2:23-24*

Paul reiterates here his uncertainty about the outcome of his trial. But Timothy's faithful years of serving God with the mind of Christ had put him in a position where Paul has no problem saying that Timothy could be his replacement.

One of the things we ought to learn from Timothy is that the mind of Christ isn't the product of a good sermon. It doesn't come from attending a week-long seminar or even a year of church. It is the fruit of a daily, committed relationship with the Lord where you are constantly faithful in doing the little things that He gives you to do in preparation for the big things that lie ahead.

"I don't have anyone but Timothy," Paul said. This encourages me because in looking to find help that shares your heart and vision you quickly discover they are never easy to find. In 30 years, Paul had one. He had a lot of men that worked with him. He had Silas and he thought the world of Epaphroditus. But he said, "I will send Timothy." I guess you ought to be grateful when you find one faithful man that can share your heart.

As Christians, you and I have to be disciples in training and, at the same time, be training others to go where we have been. On the one hand, give out what you have been given. On the other hand, receive what you have yet to learn so that you might one day be ready for whatever God has for you. You never know what God has planned, so you want to be ready.

*Yet I considered it necessary to send to you Epaphroditus, my brother, fellow worker, and fellow soldier, but your messenger and the one who ministered to my need;*

—*Philippians 2:25*

Having pointed to Jesus as the first and ultimate example of a life of service, followed by his own life and that of Timothy, Paul now points to Epaphroditus as a fourth example of "letting this mind be in you that was also in Christ Jesus." Paul was Hebrew through and through. Timothy was half-Jewish, half Gentile. From his name and his hometown of Philippi, it would seem that Epaphroditus might very well have been all Gentile. What we know for sure is that he was a young guy who volunteered to risk life and limb to carry an offering from the Philippian church to Paul in Rome some 700 miles away. No wonder Paul couldn't come up with enough good things to say about what would otherwise be an unknown saint, giving him the titles of brother, fellow-worker, and fellow-soldier. The words "brother" and "fellow-worker" literally speak of someone who was willing to roll up his sleeves and go to work next to you. The word "soldier" speaks of fighting for the faith, willing to defend the Gospel at all costs. And coming from Paul, those are high words of praise indeed.

In chapter one, where Paul was talking about the joy of the Lord, he said he loved the fellowship he had with the Philippian church (verse 5). In verse 12, he talked about the furtherance of the Gospel. Towards the end of the chapter, he talked about defending the faith of the Gospel. Here, he touches on those same three areas in describing Epaphroditus as his brother, his co-worker, and fellow-soldier. That's a good balance – one I think we need to have if we're to be useful to the Lord, because there is a tendency in all of us to lean more in one direction than another.

There are churches that are so interested in fellowship and hanging around together that they have lost sight of the fact that one of the purposes we have is to get the Gospel out. Other churches are so interested in preaching that they haven't got a clue about fellowship. They don't know each other; they don't like each other; they don't spend much time together – but they are out preaching. Then there are the folks who are always defending the Gospel but are never really sharing it. They want to fight and argue about what you do or don't believe, but they never come to the place where they want you to know that Jesus died for your sins.

Paul recognized that Epaphroditus was a well-balanced young man. When he had to defend the Gospel, he had the capacity to do so. But he was also a member of the body in fellowship and saw the need to share the Gospel with others. It reminds me of what we read about in the days of Nehemiah. There came a time in his ministry when he instructed the men who were rebuilding the wall of Jerusalem to work with a trowel in one hand and a sword in the other, in order to protect themselves from possible enemy attack. Those who balance building and defending are wise. That's the kind of man Epaphroditus was.

Paul goes on to call him a messenger. In Greek, the word is *apostolos*, a word reserved for very few. Beyond the initial 12 disciples, there are only a handful of people called apostles in the Bible and, almost exclusively, they are those who went out to pioneer new works of the church. Epaphroditus was a lot more than just a messenger to deliver a gift to Paul in prison. According to Paul, he was a missionary in every sense of the word. The phrase "one who ministered" is the word *leitourgos*, which in an Old Testament sense, speaks of one who serves in the capacity of a priest and, in the New Testament sense, of one who opened the door. In other words, Paul said, "The messenger, the missionary you sent, didn't just drop off the money and leave. He didn't just tell me about how long his trip had been and that he had better get going. He came in the form of a priest and a servant." Paul truly appreciated this like-minded brother.

❏ Day Twenty-One Complete – Date: _______________________________

Application: _______________________________

_______________________________

_______________________________

_______________________________

# Philippians 2:26-30
# Day Twenty-Two

*...since he was longing for you all, and was distressed because you had heard that he was sick.*
*—Philippians 2:26*

It is bad enough to be sick but far worse if you're far away from home. And when your sickness becomes bad enough that you may not make it, it becomes an even harsher issue. Though we're not given any details, apparently, in serving the Lord, Epaphroditus had put himself in a position to contract an illness. Yet in spite of his condition, he longed for all of them in his home church and was worried about how the saints back home might take the news of his serious illness.

The phrase "longed for" is the Greek word *epipotheo*, which means to love greatly, like you would your own children. But in this great love, the heart of Epaphroditus was heavy, *ademoneo*, so distressed that he had a hard time functioning day to day. The only other place you find this word in the New Testament is in Mark 14 with regard to Jesus in the garden of Gethsemane, facing the cross and the separation from His Father and under great duress.

Epaphroditus was physically sick and mentally down but Paul points out that he wasn't depressed about being sick or about the fact that he may not live. What he was upset about was that his family and friends in Philippi would worry about him, which meant he had to have been sick for quite some time because the trip from Rome to Philippi was 700 miles across the Adriatic Ocean. It would have taken months for someone to make the journey, find out Epaphroditus was sick, return home to tell the church to start praying, and then for word to get back to Epaphroditus that they worried about him. Still, his only concern was how his church family would handle it. It bothered him so much that he fell into an oppressive kind of depression.

How can that happen? It happens when you live for others. Here this young man volunteers in his home church to make a trip to take money to Rome to help the man who had founded the church. But in order to do that, he had to risk his neck because travel in those days was anything but safe. He probably was carrying a sizeable sum of money, as the church was going to give Paul some help. Enough to last several months, if not longer, I would guess. Epaphroditus would have to guard that money with his life. Additionally he arrived only to have to deal with illness as well. Yet he did it willingly. It wasn't an easy voyage. This same type of difficult travel had convinced John Mark to quit years earlier.

The church needs people like this – folks who are concerned enough about those in the mission field, those who are suffering hardships, those who are paying the price to get the Scriptures out – that they are willing to stand with them in difficult places. That is the kind of man Epaphroditus was. He desired to stand with Paul who was standing in a very difficult place. And I have to believe that Paul, sitting in jail and seeing Epaphroditus come all of that way with all of the risks involved, was impressed!

When we were ministering in the Philippines years ago, we couldn't drink the water anywhere. Harley, our bass player, was so sick from drinking the water that, every night we never knew if he'd be able to do a concert or have to go to the hospital again for fluids. Yet every night the Lord would get him well enough to play. He did that seven nights in a row, all because he drank some water. Yet there are missionaries that live there. How do they cope with that?

That's the kind of man Epaphroditus was. He didn't throw money in the can – he picked it up, took it with him, and delivered it himself. He showed great love for his local church as he did for the mission field. He was a balanced believer and a sacrificial one, as well, willing to give his life for the things of God.

*For indeed he was sick almost unto death; but God had mercy on him, and not only on him but on me also, lest I should have sorrow upon sorrow.*
—*Philippians 2:27*

Twice in four verses, Paul will tell us Epaphroditus nearly died, adding that it was God's mercy that raised him up and spared Paul an even greater sorrow. We can conclude that he was sick a long time – possibly 4-6 months of a bedridden type of illness. There was no immediate healing. There was no sudden work of God. In fact, for a time, Paul was in doubt as to how this might turn out as well.

Reading this story you might ask why God didn't just heal Epaphroditus immediately and miraculously. Paul had prayed for others – folks he didn't even know – and they had been healed. Yet here Paul is reduced to doing what you and I have to do when we are in that situation: praying and asking God to do a work and then waiting to see what He will do. It's a scary, heartbreaking, difficult place to be. But we shouldn't despair because we know our Lord.

God doesn't heal everyone. Nor is the prayer in faith enough to move the sovereign hand of God. God alone will choose what He does. We are given things to do: we are to lay hands on the sick and pray; we are to call for the elders of the church and anoint with oil; we are not to cease praying. But after that, we are to wait upon God. And God, being God, will have His way.

Those in the so-called "faith movement" point fingers of condemnation at people when things don't go the way they think they should. I guess they would have to point to Paul's faith, or lack thereof, as the reason Epaphroditus wasn't home in a week. Yet in so doing, they would sound like Job's counselors who spent chapter after chapter trying to dissect why God allowed Job to suffer. "I wish I knew what the reason was," Job answered, "but, regardless, I am determined that, though I rot in this flesh, I am going to one day stand before Him. He is faithful."

Job struggled with his accusers and, unfortunately, it seems that's what the faith movement so often is. It becomes the accusers of the brethren; the finger pointers who tell people they just don't trust God enough. Sure, we need to trust God more but it would be far-fetched to think that we could in any way keep God from doing what He wanted. God will have His way. If you go through the Bible, you can make a list of people who God healed that were the most undeserving people of all. I have, by experience, seen the worst sinners healed. There was a man dying of lung cancer in the hospital. His doctors gave him 6-12 hours to live – but the Lord absolutely healed him. To this day, he is still alive and he is still not saved. His son was saved and his daughter-in-law as well. We have been praying for their father for years and still he refuses Christ.

Prayer for healing can't just be a mechanical process like pressing a button. There are plenty of saints in the Bible that got sick and died. The verse about Elijah – "Elijah had become sick with the illness of which he would die" (2 Kings 13:14) – comes to mind. Hezekiah, even with 15 years added to his life, lived only to be 54. Some Old Testament believers were killed in battle, though loving God, while others died of old age hating Him. You come to the Book of Acts and you see Peter arrested with James – both of them for preaching the Gospel. James is beheaded, but before that can happen to Peter, an angel of the Lord comes and literally breaks him out of jail. James is killed and Peter is sprung. Why? Because God is God! Apparently He was done with James but still had work for Peter to do. Eventually, Peter died as well. No angel showed up to deliver him from being crucified upside down.

Should we pray in faith? Absolutely. Should we ask

God? Certainly. Should we call for the elders? We would be foolish not to if the Lord says to do so. But then, having done all, we have to rest in the Lord's care and decision-making. We sometimes balk to entrust to God something as important as our husbands, wives, and children when He may do something we don't want Him to. But He is still going to do it because He's God.

Paul says that, had Epaphroditus died, he would have had sorrow upon sorrow. Not only would he have lost a brother who had become so dear and so helpful to him, but he would know that the hearts of the Philippian believers would be broken as well. Notice that Paul says he would have had sorrow over Epaphroditus's death. I don't know why Christians think you can't sorrow over a saint who dies. Yes, the Lord rejoices in the death of the saints because they get to go home, but we sorrow because they leave us behind. Thankfully we don't sorrow like the world but we are sorrowful nonetheless.

*Therefore I sent him the more eagerly, that when you see him again you may rejoice, and I may be less sorrowful. Receive him therefore in the Lord with all gladness, and hold such men in esteem; because for the work of Christ he came close to death, not regarding his life, to supply what was lacking in your service toward me*

*—Philippians 2:28-30*

"I am sending Epaphroditus home hastily," Paul says. "It's hard for me to send him because he has been such a blessing and such a help to me. But when you see him, I know how happy you're going to be." I can just see Epaphroditus showing up at home with all of his stories and Paul's letter to the Philippians in hand.

I don't think Paul had any doubts about the kind of reception Epaphroditus would receive when he came home – all of his friends waiting at the dock to meet the boat, maybe a dinner afterwards at the home of the woman from Lydia – but he told the Philippian believers to hold him in high esteem anyway. Epaphroditus was to be highly valued not only for risking his life, but for never giving up even at the point of death.

Epaphroditus didn't slow down. He didn't take it easy. He didn't try to get out from under his responsibility. And the rules didn't change once he became sick. He supplied what the Philippians couldn't give Paul – a personal presence. Not able to come themselves, the Philippian church sent Epaphroditus. And, in love, he was a fine representative of what they couldn't do.

"For me to live is Christ, to die is gain," Paul wrote. Chapter 1 centered on a single mind as a source of joy. The result? Joy over circumstance. "Let this mind be in you which was also in Christ," he writes here in chapter 2, focusing on a submitted mind which produces joy in the service of people. And in chapter 3, we'll see a spiritual mind that will bring joy in spite of the want of things or the lack of things.

❑ Day Twenty-Two Complete – Date: ______________________________

Application: ______________________________________

______________________________________

______________________________________

______________________________________

# Philippians Three

# Day Twenty-Three

# Philippians 3:1-3
# Day Twenty-Three

Here in chapter 3, Paul turns to teach us saints that our joy is never to be dependent upon the things that we have or do not have. Instead, we have a spiritual outlook that fills us with joy – an outlook that does not fluctuate or change day to day. In the first 11 verses, Paul looks at his past life. In verses 12 – 16, he writes of his present life, and in the final five verses, he turns his eye towards the future.

Administrated by retired soldiers of the Roman army, the city of Philippi was a "Rome away from Rome." The laws were the same; the fines were the same; and the punishments were the same. And if you were fortunate enough to have been born in one of these Roman colonies, you immediately were given Roman citizenship with all of the attending rights and privileges. Paul will say to the saints here, "Just as you are citizens of Rome, you are also citizens of heaven. And though we are not yet in heaven, we are to live by those same rules." He will tell them, and us, that if we are going to have joy in the world now, we are going to have to see things from an eternal, spiritual perspective.

Even for Christians it is easy to get wrapped up in tangible things of this life: the house, the car, the clothes, the jewelry. For some it is even easier to get wrapped up in some of the intangible things of this world: power, prestige, and fame. But whether tangible or intangible, Paul wants to talk to us about how we treat things in light of our calling to be a godly people in a lost world. As believers, you and I can have tremendous joy despite the things that we may or may not possess on a worldly level because we are currently in our home away from home. We're the body of Christ. We're the people of God. We're those in whom He has begun a good work. He is coming to gather us to Himself very soon. Our perspective is vital and is gained by God's Word to us.

Paul had known the Lord some 30 years by the time he writes this letter and concludes that there are really only two ways to live in relationship to God. Either you depend upon yourself and the things you have done and seek to come to him with a self-righteous résumé and a list of accomplishments, or you come by faith in the work of Jesus for you. For those of us who have come to Jesus, our view of this life and the stuff in it drastically changes the day we surrender to Christ. So Paul speaks of the joy we can have, even if we seem to possess little in this short time we are here in the world.

> *Finally, my brethren, rejoice in the Lord. For me to write the same things to you is not tedious, but for you it is safe. Beware of dogs, beware of evil workers, beware of the mutilation! For we are the circumcision, who worship God in the Spirit, rejoice in Christ Jesus, and have no confidence in the flesh,*
>
> *—Philippians 3:1-3*

Paul says "finally" – but he's only halfway done with the letter. It is a Pauline trait to get a second wind as he shifts gears to address the big issue in the first-century church: the Judaizers, those who entered the church and turned the focus from faith in Jesus to works and practices rooted in the law. This required trusting in our flesh to do things for God. Paul begins by telling the Philippian believers to rejoice in the Lord, period. Now, there are many situations in your life that are not necessarily joyful. However, if you have a spiritual outlook, you know that if God is still on the throne and He is still watching over you that even though what you face is difficult, your joy can be in the Lord, His nearness, His presence, and His purpose for you.

I'm reminded of Jehoshaphat leading the people against a three-nation confederacy in 2 Chronicles and how the Lord told him not to worry, that they would be victorious. The army of Israel believed the word from God and went singing into battle. The fight before them wasn't a joyful prospect yet they had joy in the Lord. And that's Paul's point in this entire chapter – to filter everything through a spiritual outlook. The flesh is of little value in the long run and neither are the things of this world.

Apparently Epaphroditus had brought some questions to Paul from the church that he now seeks to answer. So before he gets to verse 2, he tells the Philippian church that he doesn't mind having to review for them the problems with the teaching of the Judaizers. This tells me that growing up spiritually takes time. One of my greatest frustrations as a young Christian was that I thought I should learn everything right away. So I would go to church and take good notes. I would study them like crazy, and then put them away and forget everything I had just read. It was in my head but had not made that long 18-inch trip to my heart for permanent residence. The best teacher is repetition. You learned the alphabet and your phone number by repetition. Paul says, "It's all right with me if I have to tell you again about these misled and often false teachers." There is something good about hearing the truth repeated. Constant Bible exposure is always beneficial.

In verses 2 and 3, Paul gives the Philippians three "bewares" and contrasts these with three descriptions of a true believer. Judaizers were both Jews and proselytes who had Judaism in their background. When the Gospel began to be preached, Judaizers mixed their faith in Jesus with their religious practices and basically undermined faith by emphasizing works. They wanted to believe in Christ as the Messiah without letting go of all of the laws that accompanied their standing as Jews. And they were so vehement about this that they demanded that any Gentile who desired to be saved must first become a Jew in practice. From there, he could get to Jesus, but he couldn't go to Him directly. In fact, the big meeting in Acts 15 was called specifically to address this very issue. I guess today's equivalent would be people teaching that you could only be saved if you got saved in their church, or you are not saved unless you are baptized! Really?

Works-based religion was something Paul had to battle with constantly and is something you and I will also have to confront as we share the Gospel with others. The natural man has the tendency to think that getting to heaven requires his own effort. It is often the only lie the enemy needs to tell to secure a soul in darkness. However, the Gospel alone can deliver us from self to faith in Jesus.

After the resurrection, Jesus first sent the Gospel to the Jews. When Peter stood up to speak to the group that was gathered in the temple after the healing of the lame man in Acts 3, he said to them, "To you first, God, having raised up His Servant Jesus, sent Him to bless you, in turning away every one of you from your iniquities" (Acts 3:26). Paul wrote to the Romans in chapter 1 that he wasn't ashamed of the Gospel; that it was the power of God to salvation to everyone that believes – to the Jew first. In fact, if you read through the book of Acts, the first seven chapters are an account of the Gospel going exclusively to the Jews. Chapter 8 is a transition chapter where the Gospel goes to the Samaritans, the "half-Jews." And it isn't until chapter 10 that the Gentiles get to hear it for the first time from Peter at the house of Cornelius. Yet when the Gospel was preached to the Gentiles and many received Jesus with open arms, it upset many Jews who had been taught exclusivity, not inclusiveness, as God's heart for all man. It took Peter three visions, two days on the road, and a houseful of Gentile Christians, for him to say, "Then Peter opened his mouth and said: 'In truth I perceive that God shows no partiality. But in every nation whoever fears Him and works righteousness is accepted by Him'" (Acts 10:34-35).

In Acts 11, when Peter and his team returned to Jerusalem, they were called on the carpet immediately to explain what had happened at the house of Cornelius. "What are you guys doing?" the church leadership asked. "It's right there in the law, page 11: Don't go into a Gentile home." But by the time Peter laid out all that had happened, the counsel could only conclude that God was now saving Gentiles, as well, by His grace, and that since they themselves could not keep the law on their own, neither would God require it of the Gentiles. The majority of the church, however, continued to fight against that understanding of grace, which led to the council meeting of Acts 15 where the only issue on the table was: How do Gentiles get saved? All the big names were there to testify and James, the pastor in Jerusalem, oversaw the discussion, and eventually stated the conclusions based on God's Word and work.

The counsel's determination was that there were to be no rules laid upon the Gentiles because salvation is purely by grace. So for many, the issue was resolved. Yet the dissenters continued to resist to the point that the church was divided between those who held the position of the apostles and those who wanted to mix the Law with the Gospel. When Paul started preaching from city to city, Judaizers followed him, telling new converts they had to observe the feast days, learn Hebrew, and be circumcised. Paul wrote his letter to the Galatians for the singular purpose of denouncing these false teachers, who mixed grace with works, and who sought to convince people that the blood of Jesus was not enough to save them.

We fall prey to this same attack whenever we are saved solely by God's grace but eventually feel we have earned our salvation because we have prayed harder, come to church, or been faithful. We move away from the Gospel anytime we forget that we don't deserve anything; that it is only by the grace and mercy and goodness of God that we are saved.

"Beware of the dogs," Paul writes. Jewish legalists called Gentiles "dogs." There were no pet dogs in those days. Dogs were wild and dangerous. That is the way Paul described the Judaizers who came into town. He warned the church to beware of those evil workers. The Greek word for evil is *kakos* and means to be wicked from within. Paul's reference is to the fact that anything added to the truth of salvation by faith is an evil doctrine. He also called them mutilators, *katatome*. It is the only place in the New Testament that this word is used, but it is used a couple of times in the Greek Old Testament, the Septuagint, to speak of the heathen who, like the prophets of Baal in Elisha's day, cut themselves in their worship of their false gods.

"Beware of the dogs, the ones who work evil, the mutilators," Paul cries in strong language. Their demand that the Gentiles first be circumcised to be saved was equivalent to the heathens cutting themselves with knives. It wouldn't accomplish anything because the Old Testament rite of circumcision had been fulfilled at the cross.

To Paul, what had been a physical sign of the covenant made with Abraham in the Old Testament became a picture of a life delivered from the power of the flesh. But the ritual that the Judaizers were peddling had now become an end in itself. In contrast, he said, we are the circumcision. Who? Those who worship God in the Spirit, not in the flesh, who rejoice in Jesus Christ and have no confidence in the flesh. The Judaizers insisted that they were the only true believers because they had been circumcised and were following the Law. Paul said the true believers were those who worship the Lord in spirit – not through works, but by faith – and rejoice in Christ Jesus.

The word "rejoice" is the Greek word for "brag" or "boast." What happens when you start trying to work your way to heaven? Whom do you boast in? You boast in yourself. You start to say, "I have been circumcised. I have been to church. I have been baptized. I have had my holy communion. I have done great things." But when you are truly saved, the only Person you can brag about is Jesus. The only thing you can say is, "I have nothing to offer God except my sin."

Jesus told a parable in Luke 18 about a Pharisee and a publican who both showed up at the temple at the same time to pray. Jesus said the Pharisee "prayed with himself," saying, "God, thank You that I am not like other men. I am not an extortioner. I am not unjust. I'm not an adulterer and I don't even look like that publican over there. I fast twice a week. I give tithes of everything I own." That was his prayer, but according to Jesus, he was only talking with himself. The publican, on the other hand, stood afar off. He wouldn't even so much as lift up his eyes to heaven. He smote himself on the breast as a sign of his unworthiness and said, "God, be merciful to me, a sinner." Jesus said the publican, not the Pharisee, went down to his house justified, for everyone that exalts himself will be abased and he that humbles himself will be exalted.

That is why Paul said the true circumcision are those who have no confidence in their flesh. The truly circumcised are those whose flesh has been cut away by faith in Christ and the only thing they are trusting in now is Him. Having said that, Paul goes on to use himself as an example.

❏ Day Twenty-Three Complete – Date: _______________________________

Application: _______________________________

_______________________________

_______________________________

_______________________________

# Day Twenty-Four

# Philippians 3:4-12
# Day Twenty-Four

*...though I also might have confidence in the flesh. If anyone else thinks he may have confidence in the flesh, I more so: circumcised the eighth day, of the stock of Israel, of the tribe of Benjamin, a Hebrew of the Hebrews; concerning the law, a Pharisee; concerning zeal, persecuting the church; concerning the righteousness which is in the law, blameless.*

*—Philippians 3:4-6*

Here, Paul meets the Judaizers on their own turf. These folks, who wanted to count religious performance as righteousness and taught others to do the same, now get to hear from someone who at one time felt just like they did. In this autobiographical section, Paul doesn't preach from an ivory tower. He says, "Look, I lived that life and I had more to be proud of than you will ever have. If it is good works, religious status, and religious accomplishments that you want, I win!"

Most of the Judaizers were Gentiles who had converted to Judaism and fell in love with the ritualistic aspects of that faith. When Paul says he was circumcised on the eighth day in accordance with the Genesis 17 covenant given to Abraham, it was an accomplishment hard for them to match. Not only that, but being of the stock of Israel meant that he hadn't converted to Judaism – he was born into it. But that's not all. He was from the tribe of Benjamin. This doesn't mean much to us but it did to the Jews. Along with Joseph, Benjamin was Jacob's favorite of his 12 sons, born to his favorite wife, Rachel. Much later in Israel's history, when Absalom rebelled, it was

Benjamin who stayed faithful to David, Israel's greatest king. Later, when the kingdom split, it was Benjamin, along with Judah, that remained faithful. So Benjamin, the tribe of Paul's lineage, was held in high honor by the Jews.

Paul continues by saying he was a Hebrew of Hebrews, which would appear to mean that both his dad and mom were Jewish. They were committed to the point that, though he was born in Tarsus, they sent him to Jerusalem to be taught by Gamaliel, the pre-eminent Jewish scholar of the day. Paul had been at it since he was a kid. When he grew up, he joined the radical movement of the Pharisees. Pharisees were fundamentalists who followed the opinions of the Rabbis that were written in the Talmud and lived out every detail of the Old Testament law as they saw fit to interpret them. Jesus repudiated them as works-oriented, ignorant of sin, and internally wicked. But outwardly, they appeared to be as holy as could be.

Concerning zeal, Paul killed Christians – which made him not only a fundamentalist but a fanatic. "You want to brag about being righteous?" Paul says. "I was so convinced I was right that I killed people and thought I was doing God a favor." The Judaizers were boasting about their passion but they couldn't compete with Paul's. Yet as a Pharisee Paul was lost and needed to be saved. So he continues…

> *But what things were gain to me, these I have counted loss for Christ. Yet indeed I also count all things loss for the excellence of the knowledge of Christ Jesus my Lord, for whom I have suffered the loss of all things, and count them as rubbish, that I may gain Christ*
> *—Philippians 3:7-8*

One day while Paul was on the road to imprison more Christians, Jesus stepped into his life and he was immediately and dramatically converted. He abandoned any notion that his work or pedigree had prepared him to stand before God. In fact, as he added up everything – which would have impressed the Judaizers – he realized his assets were actually liabilities to being saved. While he was trusting in himself, he couldn't trust in God. The way this is written in Greek, the word "gain" is plural and the word "loss" is singular. So Paul says all of his so-called gains added up to one big loss.

Paul writes this letter 30 years after being saved and note that his outlook 30 years later is still the same. When you get saved, one of the things you realize fairly quickly is that you have nothing to offer God but your trust in His work for you. You don't bring anything to the table but you. And then you hope God will take you. Once Paul was saved he had only one agenda: to know Jesus better. And he was willing to give up his advantages, his schooling, his prestige, his favored status, his pedigree, his future, his smiles from the Pharisee counsel, his position in the Sanhedrin, and his power base to that end. In fact, for him, anything else was just a big waste of time.

> *...and be found in Him, not having my own righteousness, which is from the law, but that which is through faith in Christ, the righteousness which is from God by faith; that I may know Him and the power of His resurrection, and the fellowship of His sufferings, being conformed to His death, if, by any means, I may attain to the resurrection from the dead.*
>
> *—Philippians 3:9-11*

Before I was saved, I was confident I was going to heaven because I could always find a group of people worse off before God than myself. Every time I did something better than someone else, they would go down the ladder and I would go up. So Paul could read the 10 commandments with pride, knowing he kept them all – at least he thought so until he considered the last one which speaks of not coveting, the only commandment that specifically addresses an attitude of the heart. In Romans 7, Paul writes that his self-righteousness hit an iceberg because coveting dealt with his heart, and not his behavior, and he did not know how to change his heart. Jesus, however, kept all of the commandments. He could get to the 10th commandment and live. He always did that which pleased the Father. He laid down His sinless life to cancel our debt of sin. That was Paul's only hope, and eventually Paul met Jesus and learned that to be so. "All I want now is to know Him and to have a standing with God that comes through faith in His Son." Thirty years later Paul is still on this quest to know God better. He had met Jesus, now he wanted to know Him – and knowing Him had become his lifelong concern.

"I want to know the power of His resurrection," he writes. We all want to know that, don't we? We want to experience the life giving moving of His Spirit. But Paul wanted more than even that. He also wanted to enter into the fellowship of His suffering. You see, I don't want that! I want that first part, but I don't want the second part – and I'm not alone in that. Jesus' own family rejected Him. In John 6, many of His disciples left Him. At the cross, all men would forsake Him. The prophet Isaiah said He was despised and rejected by men (53:3). Yet Paul said, "I want to know what it means to live for Jesus even if it means being conformed to His death. Yes, I want to see His power, but I also know that I have to line up with His suffering. These want to run around and circumcise people and call that spiritual accomplishment. I just want to know Jesus."

Then Paul adds, "If by any means I might attain to the resurrection from the dead." Lest you think that Paul doubted his salvation, the Greek word for resurrection is *anastasis*. In verse 11, Paul adds the prefix *ex*, which means "out." The word *exanastasis* in the New Testament always speaks of a standing based on the work God has already accomplished for us, by dying and rising from the dead. Paul says he wants to live for Christ in such a way that his new life would bring glory to God who alone can save.

*Not that I have already attained, or am already per-fected; but I press on, that I may lay hold of that for which Christ Jesus has also laid hold of me.*
*—Philippians 3:12*

After laying the so-called pluses of his old life next to Jesus and realizing just how worthless they were, Paul now looks at his present ambition and likens it to a race. One of his favorite teaching tools is the analogy – things or ideas that we can relate to – and he uses one of his favorites here: the athlete. In the Greek games, the only requirement was that you were Greek. So runners didn't run to be qualified – they already were qualified. In other words, Paul wasn't running to be saved – for he was already saved.

I once heard a man say that an ideal was something everyone expects to honor but no one expects to attain. Paul didn't live like that. He wanted to honor Jesus by the way he lived and declares, "I'm not there yet but I'm still trying." That is an interesting thing to hear from a man who had done so much. His accomplishments could fill a book, but for Paul, they weren't enough.

One of the first things I notice reading Paul's desires here is that if you are going to run the race well, you are going to have to be driven by, what I guess you could call, "sancti-fied dissatisfaction." In other words, you should never really be satisfied with how far you have come. Paul said, "I've got this great vision that one day when people look at me they are going to be able to see Jesus. But I'm not there yet."

Many believers at some point become self-satisfied and stop running. Maybe it's because they begin to compare their progress with other runners – usually ones going slower than they are. But God doesn't call us to run the race that way. Had Paul done that, he could have been the proudest guy on the planet because no one could match his split times. The guy was constantly in training. He was older than most yet he could run faster than anyone. He was in it for the long haul and had been for years, but still wasn't satisfied. He wasn't yet perfected–a word that means matured or completed. Paul said he wasn't yet where he wanted to be. That's why he was still trying, still pressing on, and still looking ahead.

I love the fact that Paul has such an honest evaluation of himself and that his heart is still fired up to be a Christian, even so many years after his salvation. In fact, 30 years in and he is just as on fire as he had ever been. He's got a goal in mind and he's got his eye on that goal.

The phrase "but I follow after," *dioko* in Greek, means that you have an eye on that which is ahead with a view towards overtaking it. Paul says, "There's my life the way it should be. There's the goal. I'm running after it quicker than it's running away from me. I'm pressing ahead. I'm catching up. And I'm not giving up." Paul was still a hungry man, as far as wanting to win the race and be that man of God he desired.

I'm reminded of the verse where David said, "As the deer pants for the water, that's how I pant for the Lord." He wrote that years after he had come to really know the Lord. "I am as thirsty for God today as I have ever been," David said, "like a deer in the wilderness looking for a water source."

Paul, writing this letter from jail where he thought he might die, says, "I have never in my life been as hungry to get ahead in Him as I am today." He wanted to lay hold of all that God had planned for him and so he pressed on.

Why did God lay hold of you? What was His purpose in saving you? According to the Bible, His first and foremost purpose was to save you from your sin. After that, it is to make you His own and to change you into the image of His dear Son, that you might bring Him glory and honor and that He might bless your life. Paul says, "I want to follow after Jesus so I might become all that God had in mind when He saved me."

Paul saw discipleship as very personal. Consequently, there might be things in your life that God has asked you to lay aside so you can run better. One thing is for sure: if you are going to get ahead with the Lord, you are going to have to be dissatisfied with the progress you have made so far and you are going to have to be determined to catch that which lies ahead of you and not yet within reach. You're going to have to make the commitment and the effort necessary to capture those things for which God has captured you.

❏ Day Twenty-Four Complete – Date: _______________________________

Application: _______________________________________________

_______________________________________________

_______________________________________________

_______________________________________________

# Philippians 3:13-16
# Day Twenty-Five

*Brethren, I do not count myself to have apprehended; but one thing I do, forgetting those things which are behind and reaching forward to those things which are ahead, I press toward the goal for the prize of the upward call of God in Christ Jesus.*
*—Philippians 3:13-14*

If the first step in running the race well is dissatisfaction with our current progress, the second step is devotion to win the race. Potential is ruined when you think you've done enough, paid enough, tried hard enough, and that you deserve to relax. However, no one in the world would actually run a race like that – not after all of the years of effort, not after pushing themselves to the point where they are passing out at the finish line just to get there.

Paul's goal was to get to the prize. He was throwing himself eagerly into the race. "This one thing I do," he said. You will find the phrase "one thing" a lot in Scripture. Jesus said it to the rich young ruler, "One thing you lack," and that one thing – the love of his wealth – kept him from the things of God. He had done so many things well but the one thing he lacked, he wasn't willing to do (Luke 18:23), turn from his things to Jesus. When Martha got mad at Mary for sitting at Jesus' feet, Jesus said, "Martha, one thing is needful – fellowship with Me" (Luke 10:42). David wrote in Psalm 27, "One thing have I desired of the Lord and that's what I'll seek after: that I can dwell in the house of the Lord all the days of my life."

Paul said, "I'm not there yet, but this one thing I do."

You have to wonder sometimes if the reason we make such slow progress as Christians is due to the fact that we can't say, "This one thing I do." Most believers are involved with so much that their walk with the Lord is just one of many things on their to-do list. If you ask them if they've been reading their Bible, they say they've been very busy. If you ask them if they've been going to church, they say their schedule is full. If you ask them if they've shared the Gospel with anyone, they say they'd love to if only they had the time. We do a thousand things but neglect the one thing that is needful.

To an Olympic hopeful, we would say, "You had better run everyday until you are sick of running, until you are faster than anybody, and then maybe you stand a chance." But if the reply came back, "I already am training. I run two blocks every other month. Now would you give me some money and support me?" we would think he was crazy. Yet what we think is so ridiculous when we talk about an Olympic athlete makes perfect sense to us when we talk about our spiritual life. Go to church. Read your Bible every day. Get on your knees every morning. I can't believe we actually have to convince people that these are absolute necessities for their spiritual life if they are going to run well.

If we want to run the race and be all that God desires us to be, we have to devote ourselves to the goal. If you want to be a strong man of God, what are you doing about it? If you want to please God, how are you going about it? What's the goal? How will you accomplish it? Paul was dissatisfied with how far he had come but he was equally committed to going further. "This one thing I do," Paul said. And then he listed three steps to his singular goal: forgetting those things which are behind, looking forward to the things which are ahead, and pressing on toward the prize.

It seems to me that Christians who are preoccupied with the past become slow runners. Those that seem to make the least progress are the ones who have the most trouble with what has already taken place in their life. They will bring you an entire shopping list of things that have happened to them and say, "Look at my life!"

"This happened today?" I ask.

"No, no, no. This is 40 years' worth of stuff."

They want to analyze their past, but have you ever tried running looking over your shoulder the entire time? Paul had left plenty of sin and chaos in his rearview mirror. On the negative side of the ledger, he used to kill Christians thinking he was doing God a favor. He threw people in jail, ripped up families, and took dads away from their children. If you want guilt, Paul had it. Condemnation? Fodder for the devil to beat you to death? Paul had a drawer full. Yet the only thought that he had was the tremendous grace and mercy God had shown in saving him. What might have dragged him backward instead propelled him forward.

On the positive side, by Paul's own mouth, the Gospel had come to two continents through his life. He could have looked back and thought, "Man, that's a race and a half right there! Let someone else go to Africa. Let someone else try to reach Spain. I've done my part." Yet for Paul, all that he'd done was yesterday's news. He would forget what lied behind – whether good or bad – because there was still a race to finish.

The word "forget" in the Bible means to no longer care for or be influenced by that which you are looking to no longer remember. Do you want to run a good race as a Christian? Don't let yesterday's failures keep you from running today. And don't allow yesterday's successes to keep you from trying harder now. You have got to press ahead. The race isn't over. If you are still breathing, God still has a race for you to run. Don't get stuck in the mud. Don't stumble over what's behind. Be grateful and get going.

Paul wasn't looking back. Why? Because he was too busy looking forward. What does God want me to do now? What does God have for me today? What is God's plan for me at this moment? In fact, the words "reaching forward" at the end of verse 13 refer to the runner that is stretching out to the tape. "I am going to run to hit the tape first." He was determined to run the race as hard at the finish as he did at the beginning. Dissatisfied with his past accomplishments, devoted to knowing Jesus, he ran with determination to win.

"I press toward the goal," Paul declares. And the phrase, "I press," in verse 14 is *dioko*, the same Greek word as "I follow" in verse 12. If every believer ran as hard to serve the Lord as they run to serve themselves, what an awesome church we would be! If we put as much determination and effort into building our faith as we do into building our careers, or into building our lives as saints as we do into building our bank accounts, what an awesome people we might be!

"I press forward towards the mark of the high calling," Paul writes, or literally the calling from on high. "I'm running for the prize which is the life that God has and that place of standing one day before God. I'm living for the day when I stand before Him and the rewards are determined. I want the prize. I want the reward. That is my goal. I am dissatisfied with how far I have come but I am determined not to lose."

It's such an interesting picture because Paul, as an older man, paints himself as a man with his head thrust forward, every muscle tense, pressing on to win the race. I have to believe that, for many Christians, the reason they don't grow very much or don't see much happen is because they don't have the conviction and determination to achieve these kinds of things in the Lord. Paul says here in just a few verses that if you want to run the race, it's going to take effort and perseverance, sacrifice and concentration.

In John 15:5, Jesus said, "I am the vine, you are the branches. He who abides in Me, and I in him, bears much fruit; for without Me you can do nothing." Yet that doesn't mean we don't participate. It's the work of the Lord in us, but it's our commitment to do it His way that will bring about His work.

*Therefore let us, as many as are mature, have this mind; and if in anything you think otherwise, God will reveal even this to you. Nevertheless, to the degree that we have already attained, let us walk by the same rule, let us be of the same mind.*

*—Philippians 3:15-16*

So Paul applies all that he has been saying by calling on the rest of the saints to join the race. I like the New International Version, which reads, "All of us who are mature should take such a view of things." It is a mature outlook which views the Christian life as a race to be run. And Paul's heart is to motivate us to run the race, to stir us up, and to move us on. Whether you know it or not, Christianity is not a spectator sport where you sit in the stands of the sanctuary, cheer on the message, applaud the music, and throw money at the missionary. That won't work. You are in the race. You have got to run. I can't make you go faster. But God can. I can't make you care. But He can. Come out of the grandstands and get in the race.

In verse 16, Paul tells us not to give up the ground that we have gained as believers. Don't lose the lessons you've learned. Keep in practice as you grow. Add new understanding to what you already know. It's a process. You can't just grow in big leaps and bounds. It's one step at a time. I used to think that if I prayed and God didn't answer I had prayed wrong, so I changed the wording. But I learned after awhile that wasn't true at all. I could probably mumble and be all right. Then I figured if I prayed for someone and they didn't get healed right away, I didn't have enough faith. But when I learned that was wrong, I didn't stumble over it anymore. I moved forward a little bit. That's what Paul wants us to do. Don't give up the ground you have gained and run by the rules.

In the 1912 Olympics, Jim Thorpe won both the pentathlon and the decathlon. He was the talk of the world until he was disqualified when it was discovered that he had played some semi-pro ball, which was against the Olympic rules. In his first letter to the Corinthians, Paul says, "Therefore I run thus: not with uncertainty. Thus I fight: not as one who beats the air. But I discipline my body and bring it into subjection, lest, when I have preached to others, I myself should become disqualified." (1 Corinthians 9:26-27).

In other words, it takes a lot of discipline and commitment to run by the rules. If you quit reading your Bible, you'll start forgetting what God says. If you quit praying, you'll quit depending on God. If you quit coming to church, pretty soon you won't miss it. If anything would be a warning to us maybe it would be the characters you find in Scripture who started off doing well but somewhere along the line lost their zeal, broke the rules, and stopped running. They didn't necessarily lose their salvation but they lost the opportunity to win any prizes, to get any rewards for God's glory, to become all they could be. Samson started off well enough and had a good shot at it. Lot had a great teacher and a godly uncle. Ananias and his wife, Sapphira, started off pretty good. So did a fellow named Demas who hung around with Paul. But none of them ended well.

"I want to catch up with that for which God caught me," Paul said. "I am not there yet but I am pressing ahead towards the up-calling, the tape, the prize." Dissatisfied with where he was, Paul continued to run with devotion, direction, determination, and discipline. And that's his counsel to us, as well.

❑ Day Twenty-Five Complete – Date: _______________________

Application: _______________________________________

183

_______________________________________

_______________________________________

_______________________________________

# Day Twenty-Six

# Philippians 3:17-21
## Day Twenty-Six

*Brethren, join in following my example, and note those who so walk, as you have us for a pattern. For many walk, of whom I have told you often, and now tell you even weeping, that they are the enemies of the cross of Christ:*

*—Philippians 3:17-18*

In verses 2 and 3, Paul had warned the Philippians about Judaizers – those who mixed the Gospel with the Law – including the Old Testament dietary laws and the rite of circumcision. It could be that here in verses 18 and 19, he is speaking about these same men. It is also possible that he is speaking about another group that was really difficult to deal with: Libertines, who believed that being free in Christ meant they could do anything they wanted. That's just like us, isn't it? One minute we are delivered from the bondage of the Law and we're praising God that we don't have to live by a bunch of rules. The next minute, we're living large in sin, proclaiming to be a Christian. Another minute and we are making rules for others ourselves.

Judaizers and Libertines have both missed the truth of God. Paul would write in Galatians 5:1, "Stand fast therefore in the liberty by which Christ has made us free," and 12 verses later write, "For you, brethren, have been called to liberty; only do not use liberty as an opportunity for the flesh," True Christianity will always be found in the majority of the believers and not ever amongst these fringe movements that are loud but in the minority. Peter said in 2 Peter 1:20 that no prophecy is open to any private interpretation. In other words, nothing God has said will come to a point where you are the only one who understands it correctly. The majority of the saints will come to the right conclusion. Paul's warning is: "You have to know that these fringe dwellers – the legalists and liberty fighters – are wrong in their assessment of the Scriptures. Follow our example. Find others like us."

As the Body of Christ, we are still faced with these two errors. On the one hand, there are Judaizers who have a rule for everything – from the way you dress to the way you pray to the type of Bible you read and whether you can sing contemporary praise music or not. Then there are those who, in the name of freedom, divorce their wives, cheat on their taxes, and go 80 mph with a "Honk if you love Jesus" sticker on their bumper. Paul said, "Those guys aren't mainstream believers in Jesus. They are the fringe groups. Be careful of them. Be followers of me."

What broke Paul's heart wasn't so much that he had to warn the saints, but that there were many who walked that way – people in church pretending to be something they weren't. Paul warned the saints, but he wept for the deceivers, because their lifestyle and beliefs put them in direct opposition to the cross of Jesus.

What is the cross? For you and me, it is the center of everything we believe. It is God's solution for our sins. If you are an enemy of the cross, then you must teach that Jesus' death isn't enough to pay for your sins or that you can follow Jesus without being accountable for the blood He shed. But if you are a friend of the cross, your life is only interested in spiritual things and the truth of God's grace and mercy, found at Calvary, which will save us and change us.

> *...whose end is destruction, whose god is their belly, and whose glory is in their shame — who set their mind on earthly things.*
>
> *—Philippians 3:19*

In Galatians 5, Paul said they who are Christ's have crucified the flesh of the affections and lusts and now live in the Spirit. Why were those in Paul's day enemies of the cross? Because they were still living for their flesh. They said they loved the Lord but they put the things of the world first. That is why Paul describes them in verse 19 as being earthly-minded. When he says their end is destruction, the word he uses is *apoleia*, "perdition." "Perdition" is the word Jesus used to describe Judas (John 17:12). It's a word used in the Scriptures almost exclusively to define the eternal death suffered as a result of the judgment of God for a failure to believe in His Son. No wonder Paul wept.

Instead of striving to keep their flesh in check, these guys found ways to make their faith bless their flesh. Aren't your greatest battles fought with your own flesh? We are constantly battling to do the right thing over the wrong thing. That's the work of God's Spirit. But that wasn't the case with these enemies of the cross. Though they were in the church physically, their minds were not tied to spiritual things at all. Yet how far removed is their message from ones often preached today in the name of the Lord? "Brother, if you just had more faith, you could live like I live. If you could just believe more, you could have what I have."

There are doctrinal positions espoused by people today who will tell you that if you truly love Jesus, you will always be healthy; you'll always be wealthy; you'll always get what you want. But these health and wealth doctrines don't fly very well in India or in the Philippines or in China, where Christians are barely getting by and are literally thanking God for their daily bread. Paul goes on to say that such people glory in their shame. In other words, they eventually begin to take pride in the very things that ought to make them sick. They live in sin and boast about it as freedom.

*For our citizenship is in heaven, from which we also eagerly wait for the Savior, the Lord Jesus Christ, who*

*will transform our lowly body that it may be conformed to His glorious body, according to the working by which He is able even to subdue all things to Himself.*
—*Philippians 3:20-21*

"Follow our example," Paul said in verse 17. Then in verses 18 and 19, he contrasted that with those who walk after the flesh. In verse 20, he picks up where he left off in verse 17, saying "our citizenship is in heaven."

I live on the earth but I am a citizen of heaven. My name is in the Book of Life. Through no merit of my own, I am a child of God, marked by His Spirit. I belong to the household of God, and I am heading home. I am obligated as a Christian to live a life that reflects that. Paul says, "We are not like those who proclaim to be Christians yet lay heavy laws on others and yet allow themselves freedoms God wouldn't allow. We are to seek to live a life that defines us as His people, living in a world that we don't belong in, looking for Jesus each day. And every night when we go to bed, our tent moves a day closer to home."

You're a whole lot closer to heaven as you read this than you were when you first got saved. But living every day for Jesus, knowing this isn't our home, will change the way you live. It will change what you say. It will change what you do. It will change what you take pleasure in. It will change how you spend your time. It will affect how you spend your money and your energy. Everything changes when you realize where you are headed.

At 90 years of age, John wrote, "And everyone who has this hope sin Him purifies himself, just as He is pure" (1 John 3:3). You'd hate for the Lord to come while you were doing the wrong thing, yet it is hard to be looking for Jesus if your God is your belly, or if fleshly interests drive your life. It's hard to go to church when you are really not interested in spiritual things. Imprisoned in Rome, Paul says to the Philippian believers, "We stand and wait for the Lord to come. That's where joy is found."

Paul says we look for our Savior and, when He comes, He will change our lowly bodies. Because of sin, we now suffer the consequences of sin. Our bodies are weak; we get sick; we age; we lose our good looks. We slowly lose the ability to do things we loved when we were younger and, if we wait around long enough, our bodies will just stop working altogether.

Yet when Jesus comes, we will get new bodies. He's going to give us one like His own. Remember what His was like? He could pop in and out of rooms. He was there; He was not there. He was visible; then He wasn't. His body was the same, but different – made for eternity. In 1 Corinthians 15:52, Paul said he would show us a mystery, that we wouldn't all sleep but would all be changed in a moment, in the twinkling of an eye. To the Thessalonians, he said that we who are alive and remain, will be caught up together with them in the clouds to meet the Lord in the air (1 Thessalonians 4:17). How is God able to give us new bodies? Paul says He is going to do it through the same power by which He subdues all things to Himself or literally the energy of His power.

No wonder Paul says, "Brethren, you have got to follow us and those who live like us. You have got to have your life and citizenship in heaven. Look for Jesus. He is the One who is going to come and give you eternal life and a body that matches His by His power."

What you truly believe will dictate the way you live your life. The things that are the most important will surface. There is no way to lie about that. It just comes out in everything you do and pursue and say. If your life is the flesh, I don't care how spiritual you make it sound, you are living for the flesh. Everyone sees it. You know it. God knows it. If your God is your belly, it shows. That's why Paul gives this warning.

Whether you find yourself caught up in legalism or in the freedom you think gives you the right to do whatever you want, be careful, because soon the Lord will come. And those that belong with Him will be seen clearly while the rest will end in destruction. I think it is a warning we need to take seriously in America because we are weak and our commitment is pretty poor. Many call upon the name of the Lord and then live like they never knew Him. That is a dangerous place to be.

Imprisoned in Rome, Paul says joy is to be found not in the flesh or in the things of this world but in looking for Jesus and living for Him each day.

❑ Day Twenty-Six Complete – Date: _______________________________

Application: _________________________________________________

___________________________________________________________

___________________________________________________________

___________________________________________________________

# Philippians Four

# Day Twenty-Seven

# Philippians 4:1-5
# Day Twenty-Seven

What began as a thank-you letter from Paul to the church at Philippi for their continued fellowship and support became one of the greatest teachings on joy in all of Scripture. In chapter 1, Paul talked about having a single mind so that, despite the circumstances in our lives, we can live for the Lord. In chapter 2, he talked about the joy that is found by having a mind submitted to doing the will of God. In so doing, no one could steal our joy. In chapter 3, he shared with us about having a spiritual mind that placed proper value on things and so keeps us joyful whether we have much, little, or nothing at all. And here in chapter 4, Paul will speak of the joy that comes from a secure mind in the Lord, one that is free from worry and resting in His oversight and care. What a chapter this is and how we need to know it well!

If I told you that you need never worry again, what would your response be? Amazement overshadowed with cynicism? Would you laugh and wonder what was wrong with me? Well, it's true. As a child of God you never need to worry. Yet in order to accomplish that outlook, you have to be willing to live a life that agrees that God is in control of everything and His will is best and is perfect for your life. Writing from prison, awaiting a sentence that could cost him his life, and unable to do anything about his current circumstance, including providing for himself, Paul could have worried plenty. Yet his mind and heart and thoughts and outlook were fixed on only one thing: trusting in Jesus and looking to see what He would do. And because of this secure mind-set in Christ, Paul was freed from anxious thought or worry.

The Old English translation of the word "worry" was "to strangle," which is an apt description of what worry does to us. It can make us physically sick. It will cloud our thinking and contribute to our making poor decisions. Worry kills the body as well as the spirit, which is why it is something God would have us to avoid.

From a Biblical standpoint, worry is wrong thinking, which then produces wrong feeling, and those feelings do not quickly subside. In fact it takes more than wishful thinking to get rid of this monster that tries to strangle us. In verse 7, Paul will give us some concrete steps we can take to have God's peace keep our hearts and feelings intact and free from worry. In fact, in verses 6 and 7, Paul declares that right praying will lead to right thinking (verse 8) which will then lead to right living (verse 9) which will result in peace like a river running through our lives. Isn't that better than strangulation from worry?

*Therefore, my beloved and longed-for brethren, my joy and crown, so stand fast in the Lord, beloved.*
*—Philippians 4:1*

Paul begins this final chapter with the word "therefore," which basically means "because of all I have just told you," here is what you can do!  Yet before he continues his thought, he segues to tell the Philippian believers how much he cares for them, calling them "beloved," and "longed-for brethren," and his "joy and crown." He wanted to be sure that, before any correction or counsel was given, that they knew in his heart, he was on their side.  They held a unique place in his heart. He more than liked them – he dearly loved them.

Paul models for us here the right way to bring correction to another. Knowing what to say is one thing – knowing how to say it is another and is equally important. I have more difficulty with the how than the what. What I want to come out of my mouth usually does and the idea gets across, but the manner is often a little rough around the edges. Here Paul carefully addresses the issue of division – straightforward but circumspectly, and with a great deal of sensitivity and kindness. Notice in verse 1, he even uses the word "beloved" twice.

He begins by calling upon them to "stand fast in the Lord." *Steko* is the Greek word for "stand fast" and means to persist or persevere. The Lord is coming soon but until He does, the Philippians must not be easily moved from their devotion to Him. They were to seek to do the right thing and keep doing it because wherever there is a door for Satan, you can be sure he will use it. So capitalize on what God has given each of you, take advantage of your position, and stand firm in the Lord.

*I implore Euodia and I implore Syntyche to be of the same mind in the Lord.*

*—Philippians 4:2*

"Implore" in Greek is the word for coming alongside, *parakaleo*. Paul, speaking to these two ladies in the church, comes alongside them, asking that they be of the same mind in the Lord. They should think the same thoughts, show the same wisdom, and rely on Him together. From all we can gather here, Euodia and Syntyche were not new to the church in Philippi. They were women of stature and reputation. They were ladies upon whom the body looked with respect and honor. But the feuding that had gone on between them had grown ugly and destructive, to the point that it was affecting not only their lives but also the life of the church in general. Others were being dragged into taking sides in the dispute.

If you have been around the church for any length of time, this story won't sound too unfamiliar to you. You know that one of the enemy's chief tools in opposing God's people and making them ineffective is division. That's how he works. I have seen it often enough. Words are exchanged between brethren and it is often over something of little value. Yet as time passes and the feud does not, soon no one is talking and battle lines are drawn. Interestingly, it is seldom, young Christians that face these disputes, for their hearts are often soft and forgiving and kinder. More often it is those we look up to and who ought to know better – far better! So, out of that conflict, the story gets told and retold to whoever will listen and sympathizers are recruited on both sides and no one is standing fast in the Lord. Paul says, "Don't do it. Instead, hang in there with Jesus by having the same mind."

The problem was serious enough for Paul to mention these two ladies by name in a letter, which according to common practice, would have been read aloud to the entire congregation and often to other nearby congregations as well. Can you imagine that? You are at Sunday morning service, listening with the whole congregation to every word from Paul – when you hear your name linked to a rebuke. Ouch! Paul had already alluded to this problem earlier in the letter (1:27, 2:2, 2:20), but who would have expected him to name names? I'm sure that Euodias and Syntyche didn't! Paul tells them flat out: "I love you but this has got to stop."

As you read through God's Word, one of the things God never asks of us is to have the same mind when it comes to fashion, food, or music. We are not called to worship in the same manner or to have the same political views. But we are commanded to have the same mind about the essential doctrines that bring eternal life: the cross, the blood of Christ, the resurrection, His deity, and that His Word is free from error. Also, we are called to forgive, to die to self, to put others before ourselves, and to these things we are called to agree together. They are the fundamental truths of Christianity. When there is an issue outside of the basic fundamental truths, we are free to disagree agreeably. When we cannot accomplish this, not only does it break God's heart but it greatly affects Jesus' cause through out the church. For this reason, Paul says it must stop.

*And I urge you also, true companion, help these women who labored with me in the gospel, with Clement also, and the rest of my fellow workers, whose names are in the Book of Life.*
—*Philippians 4:3*

Paul knew that it wasn't going to be enough to simply tell these two ladies to desist. So he calls upon his true companion—one who was bound to him in the work of the Gospel. Whether this was a reference to Epaphras or another member of the church we cannot determine. But we do learn here that Euodias and Syntyche had served with Paul in the work of the Gospel beforehand. They had been used greatly by the Lord, but now needed some help themselves. Their wounds were real and it had apparently been a lengthy, acrimonious division that had left scars.

Paul knew these ladies were saved and that their names were written in the Book of Life. The fact that they were going to heaven was of greater importance than any differences they might have had. They were both God's kids, but at this point, they were both letting sin get the upper hand.

I don't know if, while you are reading this, you might find yourself in a similar situation. Perhaps you have a grudge against someone and you are grinding your ax. Perhaps you're gathering support and there's a whole lot of whispering going on. Maybe you feel justified and have convinced others of the same. I would tell you to knock it off. It isn't worth winning that fight because it's really only the enemy who wins.

*Rejoice in the Lord always. Again I will say, rejoice!*
—*Philippians 4:4*

Paul told Euodia and Syntyche to stop arguing and start rejoicing instead. Notice he repeats himself because I think he knew what their response was going to be. Overcome by petty hurts and selfish interests, it's hard to refocus on the Lord.

Life can certainly be grim at times and we all face burdens we believe may overwhelm us, sorrow that seems to choke the life from us, or remorse that torments us. We may wonder what God's answer is for that. Paul says here you can begin by rejoicing in the Lord. Ultimately, this is the answer. If God works everything together for good, if He is in charge, and if we are going to heaven, we can rejoice in the Lord no matter what! If, for some reason, we find that we can't rejoice, it is because we haven't let God have this part of our life. We might have given it to Him once, but have since taken it back, because if we are truly in His hands, there is no one and nothing that can steal away our joy in Him.

*Let your gentleness be known to all men. The Lord is at hand.*

*—Philippians 4:5*

Paul implies that, up to now, these two sisters who had been fighting were known more for their stubbornness and selfishness than the gentleness of the Lord. What people should be seeing in them is patience, forbearance, and gentleness. After all, the Lord is at hand, Jesus is coming. Do they honestly want Him to find them in their current state?

What wise counsel. Knowing that Jesus is coming will inspire us to live godly lives. We can't leave conflicts unresolved. We must not feel comfortable with our sins. Paul asks these two ladies to stand fast and to have the same mind in the Lord. He calls upon the brethren to help them to accomplish that. Let's be peacemakers because the Lord will be here soon.

❏ Day Twenty-Seven Complete – Date: _______________________

Application: _________________________________________

_________________________________________

_________________________________________

_________________________________________

# Philippians 4:6-10
# Day Twenty-Eight

*Be anxious for nothing, but in everything by prayer and supplication, with thanksgiving, let your requests be made known to God; and the peace of God, which surpasses all understanding, will guard your hearts and minds through Christ Jesus.*

*—Philippians 4:6-7*

What more can we worry about? This is not a new command from Paul, for Jesus taught the exact same thing. Remember this portion of the Sermon on the Mount?

*"Therefore I say to you, do not worry about your life, what you will eat or what you will drink; nor about your body, what you will put on. Is not life more than food and the body more than clothing?  Look at the birds of the air, for they neither sow nor reap nor gather into barns; yet your heavenly Father feeds them. Are you not of more value than they?  Which of you by worrying can add one cubit to his stature? So why do you worry about clothing? Consider the lilies of the field, how they grow: they neither toil nor spin and yet I say to you that even Solomon in all his glory was not arrayed like one of these. Now if God so clothes the grass of the field, which today is, and tomorrow is thrown into the oven, will He not much more clothe you, O you of little faith? Therefore do not worry, saying, 'What shall we eat?' or 'What shall we drink?' or 'What shall we wear?' For after all these things the*

*Gentiles seek. For your heavenly Father knows that you need all these things. But seek first the kingdom of God and His righteousness, and all these things shall be added to you. Therefore do not worry about tomorrow, for tomorrow will worry about its own things. Sufficient for the day is its own trouble."*

*–Matthew 6:25-34*

That sums it up, doesn't it? We look around us and marvel, saying, "Look how awesome is our God who created and cares for this universe!" Yet with our very next breath, we cry, "Oh, me; oh, my. What's to become of me?" God's solution is quite simple: be anxious for or over or about nothing. There is no exception to the "do not worry" injunction and there is only one cure: pray about everything.

The word "pray" in Philippians 4:6 is the general word used in the Bible for us speaking to God and it always implies the idea of worship. When this word for prayer is used, you will nearly always find attached to it an awareness of the greatness of God and the need to rest in His goodness and power. When we are worried, we are to turn to God and worship Him. We need to remind ourselves how big He is. There is nothing He can't handle.

The word "supplication" speaks of an earnest sharing of specific needs. It means laying out in detail before the Lord what is going on in our lives. Maybe you're thinking, "Wait a minute, doesn't God already know everything?" Of course He does. Our heavenly Father knows what we need before we ask. Yet we are told to come and pray, to seek and ask and knock. Since God knows all things, the logical conclusion is that prayer is not for God's benefit but for ours. We are to give Him our life and our concerns and do it with thanksgiving, knowing He will take care of everything. By prayer, I develop dependency upon God, keeping my eyes focused upward.

There is nothing more dishonoring to the Lord than when we worry and don't trust Him. He is our Father after all.

We are more important to Him than all of His creation. Worry says we discount His ability and His concern. We should do neither. We should pray! Factor God into every equation and His peace will keep your hearts and minds.

When we came to know the Lord, we found peace with God. Before then, due to our sins, we were at war with Him. Though He sought to save us, He stood apart from us because we were antagonistic to Him. But now Romans 5:1 declares that we are justified by faith and we have peace with God through our Lord Jesus Christ. Jesus' death on the cross, provided, the sacrifice that brought us peace with God. Yet here Paul is speaking of something more, not peace with God but rather the peace of God.

What do you suppose upsets God? What do you think scares Him? Perhaps the diabolical plan in hell? How about the fact that you and I don't always want to pray? Does that get Him rattled? Does anything shake Him up? Of course not. He is God. He knows everything. He is all-powerful. Nothing can rock His boat or ruffle His feathers. We are the ones who get rattled, not God. But what if we have His peace? What if we place whatever upsets us in His hands? And what if we really believe He can take care of them all? Then we have the peace of God. As we learn to pray and cast our cares upon the Lord and, with thanksgiving, hand them over to Him who rules the universe, He will fill our hearts with His peace.

As we give God our life and trust in Him, as we worship Him for who He is, as we cast our cares upon Him and stand upon His Word, He will give us His peace from disturbing thoughts, and enable us to keep our emotions under control. Our goal ought to be worship and understanding of who God is and to bring Him our every concern. The result will be that God's peace – something we don't even have the ability to fully comprehend – will guard our hearts and our minds. The next time you're tempted to start to worry, you would do well to remember this, so that you can experience the peace of God ruling in your heart.

*Finally, brethren, whatever things are true, whatever things are noble, whatever things are just, whatever things are pure, whatever things are lovely, whatever things are of good report, if there is any virtue and if there is anything praiseworthy — meditate on these things*

*—Philippians 4:8*

Paul now turns from right praying to right thinking. It interests me that in many places in Scripture the Lord tells us we have to make a conscious choice as to what we think about. We are called to be in control of what fills our thoughts. For Euodia and Syntyche, many of their thoughts had turned to vengeance, to making good arguments for their case, and to recruiting supporters. Paul tells them they must choose to think otherwise.

About 700 years earlier, Isaiah had written, "You will keep him in perfect peace, whose mind is stayed on You, because he trusts in You" (Isaiah 26:3). Here in Philippians, we read that we can consciously put our mind on good things. Scientists tell us that we can only think about one thing at a time. If you are thinking about good things, you can't be thinking about bad ones. You can be double-minded in your choices, but not in your thought processes. It's either good or bad and Paul here gives us plenty to think about.

We are to think about whatever is true. True is the opposite of false and we are to think about what we know is true as God has taught us. We are to think about whatever is honest or honorable. We should fill our minds with respectable things rather than that which is coarse or crude. We're to think about just or righteous things. We're to think about pure things. I doubt there are many things more detrimental to our life than unclean thoughts. We are to think about lovely or gracious things that are pleasing to God. We're to think about things that are of good report; things that are worth talking about, or that bless us and others. We're to think about things of virtue or praise, that which motivates us to do better. Paul gives us this list because he wants us to know we can actively assert our determination to practice right thinking. Help us, Lord!

*The things which you learned and received and heard and saw in me, these do, and the God of peace will be with you.*
*—Philippians 4:9*

Paul practiced what he preached and here he calls the saints in Philippi to follow his example so they might have that peace of God. Paul knew from his own experience God's peace came to lives whose minds were filled with godly things. "Whatever you have seen in me, do," he says. "Look at my life. See how I have learned to rejoice in the Lord always. I have spent time in prayer and kept my mind on the things that are pleasing to God. I am not asking you to do anything I myself have not already done. If you will do this, then you will be living your life the right way and the God of peace will be with you."

*But I rejoiced in the Lord greatly that now at last your care for me has flourished again; though you surely did care, but you lacked opportunity.*
*—Philippians 4:10*

Paul greatly rejoiced as well over the resurgent support the Philippians had sent his way. In the Roman Empire of Paul's day, prisoners were not cared for by the state. Food, medicine, and clothing were not provided as they are in our day. With no means of support, Paul was entirely dependent upon the Lord. And in God's perfect timing, the Philippians were moved at this time to again send aid. Thank you Jesus, cries Paul!

The Philippians had financially helped Paul several times in past years. But months and years had passed and they had stopped, no doubt unable to help. Paul said, "I know that you cared greatly for me even when you couldn't help." Yet now they could and would and he uses the phrase "flourished again," which speaks of blossoming like a flower or a fruit that is ripe. "You couldn't have picked a better time to listen to the Lord and send some help," Paul writes. "Here I was, trusting God, and there you were, a tool in His hand, coming through at just the right moment."

The topic gave Paul an opportunity to talk about prosperity and need. And as he does, I think he seeks to communicate to the Philippian believers and to us that we need to see the balance between gratefulness for those God uses and confidence that it is only God who can do the work. Thank God for the people He raises up but it is ultimately up to Him to send the right people at the right time with the right support. God knows our needs even before we know them. His plans are always fulfilled in the lives of the saints.

Joseph, for example, was sold into slavery as a 17-year-old. But, through a whole series of events, God continued to care for him to the point that, when the famine in Israel had gotten so bad they needed to go to Egypt for food, He had already made Joseph second in command to Pharaoh. The very people that had to beg for food were his brothers–the ones who had years earlier sold him down the river. It's an awesome story, full of great lessons. But there is one verse in particular that shows us Joseph knew about resting in the Lord without fear or worry. When his brothers stood before him weeping, faced with their sins of the past and fear of the future, Joseph revealed himself to them and, with great love, declared, "But as for you, you meant evil against me; but God meant it for good, in order to bring it about as it is this day, to save many people alive." (Genesis 50:20). Joseph understood the providence of God that would even turn the wickedness of his brothers for his purposes. Through it all Joseph learned God was in charge. So had Paul! So must we!

To the Romans, Paul would write, "And we know that

all things work together for good to those who love God, to those who are the called according to His purpose" (Romans 8:28). Paul believed it and had seen it and was experiencing it here again as the Philippians chose this particular time to reengage themselves in support for Paul. It was God's providence that had stirred their hearts and Paul rejoices over it!

"I rejoiced in the Lord greatly that your care for me had flourished again," Paul says. In other words, "I am so thankful that God stirred your hearts when He did. There couldn't have been a better time." The fact that he adds the words "now at the last" suggests that things were getting down to the wire, that maybe Paul had been praying for a break for some time but God hadn't seen fit to send anyone until now. "Praise His name," Paul says. "I was down to $1.85. I know that you have been concerned – you just lacked opportunity." This, by the way, is quite different from the church today, which lacks concern but has plenty of opportunity. The Philippian church had great concern – they just weren't able to do anything about it. Paul saw their coming as God's providence yet again and praised His name for it.

If you really want to learn to be content, you have to first be convinced that God is ruling your life, that nothing in your life is an accident, that you belong to the Lord, and because of that, He is guiding your steps each and every day.

❏ **Day Twenty-Eight Complete – Date:** ________________________________

Application: _____________________________________________________

# Philippians 4:11-23
# Day Twenty-Nine

*Not that I speak in regard to need, for I have learned in whatever state I am, to be content: I know how to be abased, and I know how to abound. Everywhere and in all things I have learned both to be full and to be hungry, both to abound and to suffer need. I can do all things through Christ who strengthens me.*
*—Philippians 4:11-13*

The word "need" in verse 11 is the word for "lack" or "necessity." Paul is saying, "I'm not trying to tell you that I am really hurting so that you will give more often. I am trying to tell you that God is faithful. I am not trying to tell you that your gift cheered me up because the Lord had done that already. I didn't write this to you in respect to need because my joy doesn't depend upon what you gave. I wasn't destitute. I'm not in despair. God isn't broke. I wasn't worried. He is the Lord. He used you but it was His timing that was awesome." It was such a balancing act: to thank them and yet not thank them, to bless them but to let them know that his trust was not in them but in the Lord.

"I have learned in whatever state I am to be content." Wouldn't you like to learn that? Paul could be content despite the fact that he was broke, in jail, and possibly soon to die. He had learned that he could be content whether he was traveling the world preaching – or chained to a Roman soldier in a jail cell. He was content whether he was sharing with kings – or with the slaves in Nero's household; whether he was writing a theological masterpiece like the Book of Romans – or a quick little thank-you letter to a small church in Philippi. "I'm just happy to be serving the Lord and it doesn't really make any difference to me what the outward circumstances are because my trust is in Him. I have learned there is a greater joy than what having plenty can bring. There is a greater joy for me than having a lot of extra. There is a greater joy than learning to live with nothing. The greater joy is always there. It is found in God's faithfulness."

Isn't than an enviable position – that whatever you have or don't have doesn't add to your contentment because of what you have in the Lord? Yet Paul had to "learn" to be content. Notice the word "learned." He had to learn to be both abased and to abound and still be content. I think it's easier to learn the abasing part because when you have very little, it's natural to run to the Lord for help. But abounding brings its own set of difficulties, for the natural man is never satisfied. With abounding comes pride, self-interest, and fleshly indulgence. With abounding, there is a tendency to be smug and to lord it over people and to find very little need to trust God.

I think we all think that if we had a lot of something, we could handle it. But Paul said he had to learn both sides of the fence. It's not easy to go without when others have. Neither is it easy to have a lot of things and still depend upon God for your daily needs. Where did Paul learn this? According to verse 12, everywhere, and in all things. The word "learned" in verse 12 is not the same as the word "learn" in verse 11. In verse 12 "learned" speaks of being let in on a secret. It is the Greek word for the pagan religions that would say to the world, "We know something you don't know. We have got the inside scoop on things and only we, the ones who have the secret handshake, know all about it."

Paul said, "I have learned a secret. I have learned that I can do all things through Christ who strengthens me. I can be content in Jesus because He knows what He's doing – even when I'm shipwrecked, stoned, beaten, hungry and thirsty, naked and cold (cf. 2 Corinthians 11:24-27). I learned that wherever I went, whatever I did, wherever I turned, no matter what happened to me, God was in charge. And through it all, I found the hidden treasure of being a Christian – that God can keep us where He brings us."

If you're a Christian, God isn't leaving. He's on the boat with you until you are gone. He's with you every step of the way. He knows what's happening. "Yeah, but I don't like what is happening," you say. Then just wait a bit. God is good. I assure you it is not Him that's the problem. It's not God's care for you that is lacking. He's doing fine. It's your attitude towards Him that needs fixing.

By drawing on the knowledge of God's promises and power, Paul was able to say, "I can do all things through Christ. I'm all right. I'm covered." In John 15, Jesus taught the same lesson when He said that He is the vine and we are the branches. Branches don't produce any fruit by their own effort. Their only hope is to draw life from the vine. Jesus said if we abide in Him and He in us, we'd bear much fruit. So if we stay in communion with God, the power of Jesus will keep us content despite the temperature on the outside. That's a pretty good lesson to learn, isn't it?

After talking about the over-ruling providence of God and the unfailing power of our Lord, Paul ends with the unchanging promises of God ...

*Nevertheless you have done well that you shared in my distress. Now you Philippians know also that in the beginning of the gospel, when I departed from Macedonia, no church shared with me concerning giving and receiving but you only. For even in Thessalonica you sent aid once and again for my necessities. Not that I seek the gift, but I seek the fruit that abounds to your account.*

*—Philippians 4:14-17*

If you go back to Acts 16 or so, you find that, through a whole series of events, the Lord finally got Paul to Europe. Arriving in Philippi, Paul lasted but a short while before being falsely accused, beaten, thrown in jail, and eventually chased out of town for good. But he had left behind a small church. He went down the road through Amphipolis and Apollonia before arriving in Thessalonica.

In Thessalonica, only 100 miles or so from Philippi, an offering arrived from the Philippian church. It hadn't been a month since he had been there but they had already come to help. It blesses me to see this church — so young in the Lord, yet so concerned about the Gospel going out — step up to support Paul in his ministry. Often, Paul would work his tent-making job to support himself and his team. That was his trade. But he couldn't do that in Europe, for early on he rarely stayed long enough in a town to establish work. Yet this young little church was the church that for years was Paul's only means of support in Europe. God had helped him by stirring the Philippians time and again.

Yet Paul was never one to dwell too long on the temporal side of an issue. So in verse 17, he says, "I am grateful for your help but what I am more excited about is the fact that your willingness to give might help produce fruit that God can put in your account. I am thrilled by the concept that you are going to get a spiritual reward in eternity for your faithfulness to give to the work that God has set before me."

In Proverbs 19:17, Solomon was led, by the Holy Spirit to write "He who has pity on the poor lends to the Lord, and He will pay back what he has given." In other words, when you bless God, He'll just bless you more because you can't out give Him. For that reason, Paul says, "I don't want a gift. I just want God to have a record of your giving because I know you'll be blessed for it."

*Indeed I have all and abound. I am full, having received from Epaphroditus the things sent from you, a sweet-*

*smelling aroma, an acceptable sacrifice, well pleasing to God. And my God shall supply all your need according to His riches in glory by Christ Jesus.*
*—Philippians 4:18-19*

The word "abound" in verse 18 is the Greek word for super-abundance. "I have more than I can hold," says Paul. "It's falling out of every pocket." And although that wasn't physically the case the day before, it was still true then because God was in charge of every day of his life. We get many letters each month from organizations asking the church for support or contributions. Most are from people we have never met. I know Paul would never have written such a letter. If he had a need, he told the Lord, not the Philippians. He saw their gift as a sweet-smelling sacrifice that God would accept and with which He would be well pleased. Paul wanted them to see that although they were helping him, it was the Lord they were blessing. And in turn, He would meet their needs even as He had met Paul's needs through them.

*Now to our God and Father be glory forever and ever. Amen. Greet every saint in Christ Jesus. The brethren who are with me greet you. All the saints greet you, but especially those who are of Caesar's household. The grace of our Lord Jesus Christ be with you all. Amen.*
*—Philippians 4:20-23*

Paul closes this great letter by sending his own greetings as well as those of Caesar's household. I like that! While Nero was deciding whether Paul would live or die, his servants were getting saved guarding Paul.

❑ **Day Twenty-Nine Complete – Date:** ________________________________

Application: ________________________________________________

_______________________________________________________

_______________________________________________________

_______________________________________________________

# Review
# Day Thirty

The Book of Philippians is essentially a missionary thank-you letter from Paul to the church at Philippi for their financial support of his ministry – especially at a time when, as a prisoner, he was unable to even pay for daily necessities. But as he sits to write thank you, Paul gives them and us so much more. In this letter of 100 verses or so, Paul uses the words "joy," "rejoice," or "gladness" some 19 times – odd words to find in a letter from a man on death row! I would expect rather to see words like "persecuted," "difficult," "need prayer," "send air," "plan breakout." Yet it's the joy of the Lord from which he writes, even though there is no reason in his circumstances to find it.

By the end of Acts 28, Paul is a prisoner in his own rented house. He is chained to a Roman soldier 24 hours a day and forbidden to preach in public. He has been in jail for a long time now, including a stint in Caesarea for a couple of years before even getting to Rome. He hadn't done anything wrong and still was unsure of his future. Yet out of all of that uncertainty and suffering, Paul was living a life that overflowed with joy.

As Christians who have the luxury of God's Word, we can't help but wonder how in the world he did it. I mean, what is the secret behind the kind of joy Paul had? In his letter to the Philippians, he'll use the word "mind" ten times and the words "think" or "remember" five more because the real secret to Christian joy is how we think. Our attitude or outlook often determines the outcome in terms of our joy or lack thereof. Solomon wrote in Proverbs that as a man thinks, so he is (Proverbs 23:7). But Christian joy is far more than positive thinking. After all Jesus died for us, and His sacrifice is needed by each of us.

In the four short chapters of this book, Paul gives us four areas that can rob us of joy but, if overcome by faith, can be sources of joy. For example, in chapter 1, he focuses on circumstances and how you can overcome them by having a single mindedness towards the Lord. How many things are in your control? The weather isn't. Traffic isn't. Your health, for the most part, isn't. Therefore, if you are a person who needs ideal circumstances to be joyful, you are going to be miserable most of the time. I think it was the poet Byron who cynically wrote that men are the sport of circumstance.

James would write in chapter 1 of his letter that the double-minded man is unstable in all of his ways. Paul wasn't like that. That is why, in verse 21 of chapter 1, Paul says to the Philippians, "For me to live is Christ and to die is gain." It wasn't that Paul was ignoring the truth. It's just that he looked at his difficult circumstances and said, "I am living to serve Jesus and whatever His purpose for my life is, that's fine with me. I belong to Him." So in his letter to the Ephesians, he refers to himself not as a prisoner of the Romans, but as a prisoner of Jesus Christ. Single mind, single outlook!

A lot of Christians look through their circumstances to find Jesus. Paul did it the other way around: he looked at his circumstances through Christ. He sees Jesus first and then everything else is just fine. How do you deal with circumstances and still have joy? You look to the Lord.

It interests me that our tendency is to say the Lord is in charge of our lives only when things go well. Yet if you were to get fired from your job unexpectedly, it's "I don't know what happened. Something went wrong; someone disobeyed God; Lord, where are You?" When you get sick, when you are mistreated, when you get ripped off, when your kids don't do what you want them to, God is still in charge, isn't He? What are you worrying about. You just don't like the way He is running the show. Paul said, "I'm sticking with God; I'm sticking with His commitment; I'm sticking with His faithfulness; I'm sticking with His promises. Even though I am on death row for something I didn't do, I have great joy because I am serving the Lord."

In chapter 2, Paul went from circumstances to something else that can steal your joy: people. If the key to joy in circumstances is a single mind focused on Jesus, the key to joy in the midst of people is a mind submitted to the Lord. Someone once wrote, "To be truly happy in this life, all I need is to get rid of everybody else." No doubt, all of us at some point have lost our joy in the Lord because of the behavior of others, by what they said or didn't say or what they did or didn't do. So the question becomes: As a Christian who is supposed to be walking in the joy of the Lord, how can I be joyful with all these less-than-likeable people around me?  How can I be the salt of the earth and the light of the world without the salt losing its flavor and the light becoming dim?

The solution is here in chapter 2: submit your life to the Lord and, in love, seek the benefit of others before that of your own. One thing that kept Paul rejoicing was that Paul had died to Paul. He was a yielded man who honestly couldn't have cared less about himself if it meant that you would be blessed. If we lived so that others would be happy even if it meant we might not necessarily get our way, Paul said we could have joy even when people are around. If he put Jesus first in chapter 1, he put others second in chapter 2. Paul was convinced that the good of others was more important than his own plans. And it's an attitude that I believe you rarely find.

Most people – even those in leadership – will do things to their own benefit. It if helps me, if it comforts me, if it's in my schedule, if my time frame permits, if I like it, if I'm available, if it doesn't put me out too much, hey, I'm here to serve God. Not Paul. He didn't spend five minutes in jail wondering why he was there. He said, "If this is what the Lord wants so that the folks in Philippi can be more faithful and the folks in

Rome can be more excited about Christ, fine. God, use me any way You want. I'm Yours."

In chapter 2, Paul gives examples of men who, dying to themselves, were filled with joy: Jesus, himself, Timothy, and Epaphroditus. I don't know if Paul was making outlines as he went, but he spends the whole chapter driving home the same point.

In chapter 3, Paul spends some time looking at a third potential rip-off of joy: things. He devotes himself in that chapter to discussing our need and want for things and says that we can overcome them by having a truly spiritual outlook. I read a story of a wealthy man moving into a new mansion next door to a Quaker farmer. The farmer stood at his gate and watched this fellow moving in box after box of stuff and truckloads of fancy furniture. When the unloading was all done, the Quaker fellow went over to the man and said, "If you find you need something, call me and I'll teach you how to live without it." His point was well taken; it's easy to be consumed with stuff.

The world is preoccupied with buying, getting, and collecting; with money, success, and worldly possessions. And the worst offenders are oftentimes Christians, who are really the ones who should know better. The world is out to get all they can–stuff is their god. They serve their god very faithfully, for some as much as 80 hours a week at work. But we shouldn't do that. We have a God who says that these things are just going to pass away? Didn't Jesus say in Luke 12:15 that we ought to be careful about coveting things because a man's life doesn't consist in the things he possesses? Was He lying or was He telling the truth? If He was telling the truth, why are we so hog-wild for all of that stuff?

What about all those lessons in the Sermon on the Mount where Jesus said we should lay up treasures in heaven rather than storing them on earth where they won't last, won't satisfy, and can't be taken with us? Paul spends an entire chapter talking about things and our need for a spiritual outlook concerning them. A heavenly perspective frees you from gathering and leaves you with great joy. Just imagine if the first thing on your mind each morning wasn't driven by the need to make more money and get more stuff. Jim Elliot, who died ministering to the Auca Indians said, "A man is no fool to give up what he can't keep to get what he can't lose." He was right. He gave his life, and his ministry continues to this day.

We need to have God's viewpoint and Paul lays it out in chapter 3, saying that the things of the world will only make you thirst again but spiritual pursuits will bring joy. So Paul says in chapter 1 that the way to have joy in circumstances is to have a single mind that says, "I have died and given my life to Jesus. He is Lord." In chapter 2, he says the way to have joy regarding people is to live a life of putting others before yourself. In chapter 3, he says regarding things that we should know that even believers can be robbed of joy when their whole life is governed by the things of this world.

Finally, in chapter 4, Paul addresses the last thief of joy: worry. The greatest threat to joy is worry. If Paul had wanted to worry, it seems to me he could have made a long list of things to worry about, a list that would shame our meager list of temporal concerns! He was in jail, a political prisoner accused of treason and bigotry. The church in Rome was divided about his authority and he had no financial aid or mission board to support him. Neither did he have a lawyer to represent him even though his crime carried the death penalty. It seems to me that Paul had plenty to worry about – but he doesn't worry. Why? It certainly wasn't that he had a brash, "don't worry be happy" outlook that ignores the obvious. He wasn't sticking his head in the sand and hiding from reality. He talks in chapter 4 about keeping or guarding our hearts with the security that Jesus has given us.

The word "keep" is a military word that means to stand guard like a sentry outside a residence or a gate. Don't worry, Paul says. Instead, give everything to the Lord and let Him stand outside the gate of your heart, keeping the problems at bay. In chapter 4, we see the peace of God, the power of God, and the provisions of God so that we can rest. In verse 4, Paul says, "Rejoice in the Lord always. Again I will say rejoice!" In verse 10, he says, "I rejoiced in the Lord greatly." What a happy guy. Is he serious? You bet he is.

Chapter 1 deals with circumstances; chapter 2 with people; chapter 3 with things; chapter 4 with worry. Remember those four and you will know the whole book of Philippians. And when people say to you, "I can't stop worrying. Can you help me?" you'll turn them to Philippians 4 and they'll think you're a pastor! Or they'll say, "People are really bugging me" and you'll turn them to Philippians 2. Pretty good, huh?

Circumstances, people, things, and worry. See what I mean?

❑ Day Thirty Complete – Date: _______________________________

Application: _______________________________

_______________________________

_______________________________

_______________________________

# Acknowledgements

I must first of all express my thanks to Nikki Smith, without whose vision and diligence in ministry this book would not have been made possible. Her dedication to the Lord and His Word and to me and my preaching have caused this manuscript to be what it is today. Her transcription, editing and selfless dedication to this project have been an example to all of us of how God would have us approach Him in our service.

Additionally the weekly proofreading of my secretary Susan Thomas, my wife Debbie and several of our staff pastors, Rod Harris, Lyle Phillips, and Ron Kitchell must not go without notice. Their input, prayerfulness, and commitment made my work so much easier. They are women and men dedicated to God and His people and for their fellowship and partnership I am a blessed man.

For my son Jacob Abeelen whose gifts of management and oversight, given Him by the Lord and now given back to the Lord as our Administrative pastor and director of Growing thru Grace radio, I am both a thankful pastor and proud father. He is indeed the answer to a father's prayers and hopes for his children. I trust God has great things in mind for him in the years to come. His oversight brought us all together.

Thank you to Pastor Brian Procedo for your layout and artwork. Your abilities to see what has yet to be drawn or formatted are amazing. God has certainly used you in this study guide and for that I praise the Lord for you.

Finally, to all the saints at my church, Morningstar Christian Chapel, I am so blessed to be your pastor and so thankful that God has placed you in my life. The fruit amongst us is found in the faithfulness of so many that serve the Lord without fanfare or notice, loving Him because He first loved them. In our midst Jesus is worshipped and honored. His Word is our delight and it continues to go out from this place in your lives, in our testimonies and in so many outreach ministries around the world. You are my joy in Him!